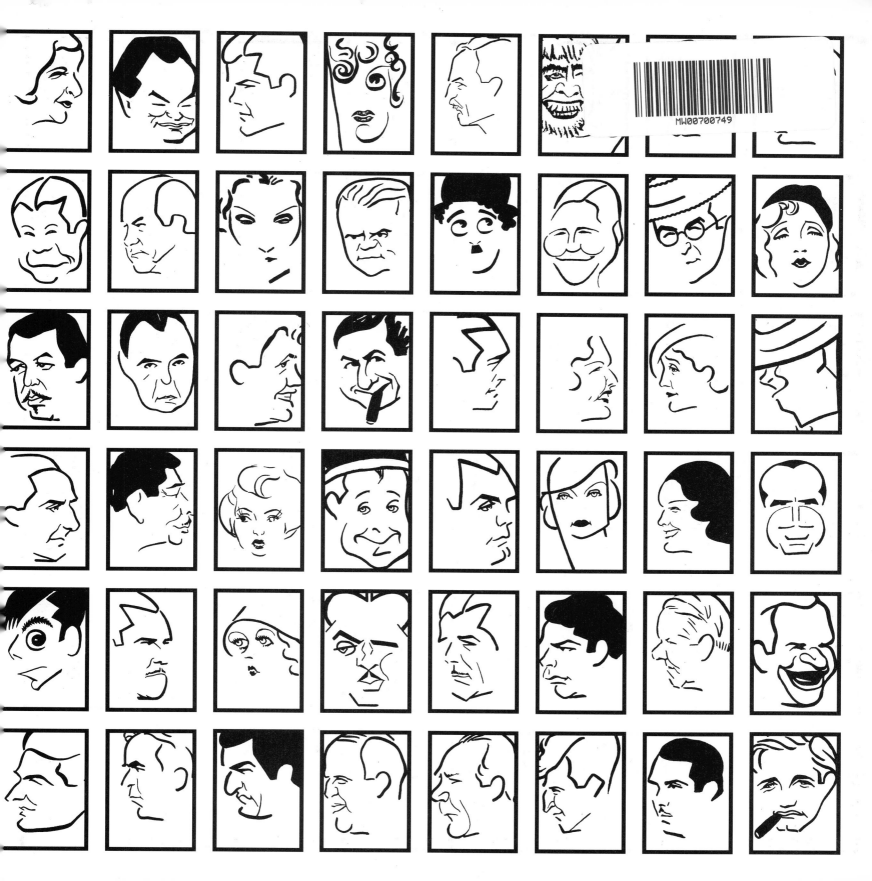

The

BROWN DERBY

Restaurant

The BROWN DERBY *Restaurant*

A Hollywood Legend

SALLY WRIGHT COBB
AND MARK WILLEMS

RIZZOLI
NEW YORK

First published in the United States of America by
RIZZOLI INTERNATIONAL PUBLICATIONS, INC.
300 Park Avenue South
New York, New York 10010

Library of Congress Cataloging-in-Publication Data

Cobb, Sally.
   The Brown Derby Restaurant : A Hollywood Legend / Sally Cobb and Mark Willems.
    p. cm.
   Includes index.
   ISBN 0-8478-1925-6 (HC)
   1. Brown Derby Restaurant (Hollywood, Los Angeles, Calif.)
   2. Motion picture actors and actresses
—United States—Anecdotes. 3. Cookery, American. I. Willems, Mark. II. Title.
TX945.5.B76C63 1996
641.5'09794—dc20   95-48891
                      CIP

Design by Big Fish Books

Printed in Singapore

CONTENTS

To my daughter
Peggy Cobb Walsh,
the light of my life.

Foreword

THE BROWN DERBY and the Hollywood that I knew are of an era that is past. I don't know what will be next, but I do know what it was like in those great days. For me, starting in 1935 and continuing for decades, The Brown Derby was home base.

For so many of us, the Derby played a central part in our lives. Hollywood was small in those days and you always ran into someone you knew at the Derby. Although you saw and were seen, that really wasn't why you went. It was for the quality of the food, the excellent service, and to see a good friend, Bob Cobb. "Bobby" was one of my closest friends; if I ever needed anything or had a problem, I'd ask Bob. I trusted him. Later when I married Ronald Reagan and Bob married Sally, we all became friends. Ron and I practically lived at the Derby—it seemed we were always there.

The Brown Derby was also a place for business. My agent would call and say, "Meet me at the Derby." If I was doing a radio show across the street at the Lux Theater, or if I wanted to have lunch away from the studio, I would stop at the Derby. It was also a family restaurant. I took the children to the Beverly Hills Brown Derby on the cook's night out. When my daughter Maureen was married, Bob brought his pastry chef out of retirement to create the last of his famous ribbon cakes for her wedding.

I am so glad that Sally has written this book because it represents a time and place that should be remembered. We are losing our landmarks, and with them we lose our heritage. The Hollywood Derby, the Beverly Hills Derby, the "Hat" are all gone. I don't know of anything like them that exists today but this book is a wonderful look at what was Hollywood.

JANE WYMAN

Introduction

WHEN HOLLYWOOD WAS IN its Golden Age, the Hollywood Brown Derby was the most famous restaurant in the world. Its enormous success was the reason that its location at the intersection of Hollywood Boulevard and Vine Streets became the symbolic as well as literal heart of the entertainment industry. The Derby had a reputation for great food, but it was much more than a restaurant—it was the real center of the glamorous film world and host to the greatest stars. It was said that everyone connected to the movies entered the Derby at one time or another.

I remember my first dinner at the Brown Derby in 1940 and the thrill of dining among the stars. I had no idea that five years later I would marry Robert Cobb, the owner of the Brown Derbies and the most charming and handsome man I would ever meet. In addition to the Hollywood Derby, Bob had the "Hat"—the one that was built to look like a huge bowler sitting on Wilshire Boulevard—and Derbies in Beverly Hills and Los Feliz. We had twenty-five wonderful years together until Bob's death in 1970. Since then, I refused countless offers to write a book about the Brown Derby and Hollywood's heyday. I changed my mind when I met Mark Willems, who has a remarkable understanding of the glamour, romance, and history that made the Brown Derby a legend.

In putting this book together, Mark and I have reviewed hundreds of photographs and endless press clippings. Many of the photographs included never have been published before and others have not been seen since they appeared in fan magazines or newspapers decades ago. Making the final selections became nearly impossible, and many of the people and stories that deserved to be included had to be left out. We have tried to capture the feeling of an era when Hollywood shaped the dreams of the world. We focused mostly on Hollywood's greatest decades, the thirties and forties, the years that the Hollywood Brown Derby was famous all over the world and was synonymous with Hollywood itself.

SALLY COBB

Mr. and Mrs. Robert H. Cobb

ℛ o b e r t   H .   C o b b

NOW *THERE* WAS A MAN! This phrase often follows any reference to Bob Cobb by those who knew him and it well describes Robert Howard Cobb. He never forgot who he was, where he was going or where he had been, or any of the people he met along the way. Everyone knew they were very special to the handsome Montana Cowboy when he greeted them with his resounding "Hi ya partner."

Bob's friendly charm, the warmth of his personality, and his gracious hospitality were as much a part of the tremendous success of the Brown Derby Restaurants as were the quality of the food, the atmosphere, and the flawless service.

Bob was the sort of restaurateur who would operate a hot dog stand with the same care and efficiency that he would exercise in handling a gourmet's paradise. As a matter of fact, that is precisely what he did. The first Derby menu was hamburgers, hot dogs, melted cheese sandwiches and chili, each prepared from the finest quality available. As the menu grew, it grew with only the best. The Brown Derby served prime eastern beef exclusively, the lobsters were from Maine, the Canadian bacon was from Canada, the cream for the coffee was heavy; even the celery was a gourmet variety—Pascal from Colorado.

Bob was, to put it mildly, a fastidious person. His attire was always in the latest fashion and impeccable, although he tempered it on occasion with a cowboy boot heel on his handmade finest of leather footwear or with his father's brand embroidered on sport shirts, where others would have a monogram.

His attention to detail was never missed in the Derbies either. . . and contributed to their incredible popularity. The tables were set perfectly and the china and silver were spotless. The staff was inspected daily and had to be immaculately groomed and there were no fraying uniforms, no missing buttons on the freshly starched linen jackets.

While my mother Sally and The Brown Derbies were certainly his first loves, a close third was baseball. In 1938, when the California Mission baseball franchise became available, Bob, along with Bing Crosby, Robert Taylor, Barbara Stanwyck, Gary Cooper, George Burns, Walt Disney, and Cecil B. DeMille invested in what became a Triple-A baseball team in the Pacific Coast League, The Hollywood Stars,

with more celebrity fans than any major league team ever. Bob was President of the Pacific Coast League at one time and helped bring major league baseball to Los Angeles.

Bob was one of the nation's great hosts, as much at home with world famous celebrities and princes as he was with the tourists who came to the Derby. As his stepdaughter, I grew up watching him hunt with Clark Gable, Gary Cooper, and Robert Taylor; shoot ducks with Bing Crosby and Phil Harris, and dance with Joan Crawford, Barbara Stanwyck, and my mother. And could they dance. While other couples preferred dancing to "Always" or "Moonlight Serenade," Mother and Bob, who could dance to anything, would Samba the night away to their favorite, "Brazil."

In an era that defined style, my mother, Sally Cobb, was known for her great style and flair. Her marriage to Bob Cobb was a perfect match. They could dance better, laugh better, stay up later and talk baseball better than most, and they understood each other's likes, wants and needs completely. Their union helped sustain the Brown Derby's thriving business for twenty-five years.

I was really lucky to have Bob as a stepfather during those twenty-five years. No father could have been more loving, caring or understanding. There was a Man.

PEGGY COBB WALSH

The Derbies

THE HOLLYWOOD BROWN DERBY

The Hollywood Brown Derby was an immediate success after its opening on Valentine's Day in 1929. Located on Vine Street, a half block south of Hollywood Boulevard, it became the hub of Hollywood, surrounded by broadcasting studios, theaters, and movie studios. The most famous of all the Derbies, it was here that movie stars, celebrities of all types, the rich, and the powerful gathered for decades.

The Hollywood Brown Derby symbolized Hollywood, and its design is part of the history of the movie capital. The architect was Carl Jules Weyl, who was responsible for many of the designs incorporated into the "Hat," the Beverly Hills, and Los Feliz restaurants. Weyl went to work for Warner Brothers as an art director when his architectural practice failed during the Depression. He won an Academy Award for the *Adventures of Robin Hood* in 1938, and as the art director for *Casablanca*, Weyl created the look and mood of another legendary restaurant, Rick's Cafe. In the classic film, Weyl created an office above the restaurant for Rick (Humphrey Bogart) as he had done years before with Bob Cobb's office above the Hollywood Derby.

THE HAT

The first Brown Derby opened on Wilshire Boulevard across from the Ambassador Hotel in 1926 during the era of silent films. It was the only one of the four Derbies built in the shape of the famous hat. The restaurant was expanded to include an open-air dining patio when it was rebuilt in 1936 at the corner of Wilshire and Alexandria, a half block from the original location.

BEVERLY HILLS

In 1931 the Beverly Hills Brown Derby opened at the corner of Wilshire Boulevard and Rodeo Drive, which became one of the most important corners in the world. A landmark in Beverly Hills for more than fifty years, it was frequented by residents, tourists, and countless celebrities.

LOS FELIZ

The last of the Derbies, it opened in 1941 on Los Feliz Boulevard and Hillhurst, in the exclusive Los Feliz section of Los Angeles. In addition to the dining room, the streamlined design of the restaurant featured the Car Cafe. This reflected the recent trend of people dining in their cars that had originated in California.

The Brown Derby Restaurant   *1628 N. Vine St.-Hollywood-Calif.*

The Hollywood Brown Derby

$\mathcal{T}$he Legend Begins

THE BROWN DERBY legend began one evening in 1925 over dinner at the Ambassador Hotel with the motion picture producer Herb K. Somborn, the great wit of Broadway and Hollywood Wilson Mizner, and theater owner Sid Grauman. Somborn was the second husband of Gloria Swanson and a man with sophisticated friends. Mizner, who later wrote the screenplay for *One Way Passage*, was as well known as his famous brother, the architect Addison Mizner. When conversation turned to opening a restaurant that would appeal to such good fellows-about-town as themselves, Wilson Mizner offhandedly remarked that if food and service were good, "people would probably come to eat it out of a hat." It was also reputed to be Mizner's idea to call the new restaurant The Brown Derby and to build it in the shape of a hat, one large enough to fit the inflated head-size of some of the movie personalities of the day.

The first Brown Derby opened in 1926 and served a few simple dishes meticulously prepared from the finest and freshest ingredients. The service was swift and flawless. The restaurant stayed open twenty-four hours a day, which was—and still is—unusual in Los Angeles, and it was a huge success. In the beginning most of the Derby's customers were men—actors, writers, artists—many of whom were from New York and knew how to live well. It was a clubroom for the old Hollywood circle headed by Mizner, writer Gene Fowler, and the Barrymore brothers, John and Lionel. Other early patrons were Will Rogers and Cecil B. De Mille, and such silent film greats as Mary Pickford, Rudolph Valentino, Mae Murray, and John Gilbert.

Bob Cobb, a young man who loved to dance, first met Herb Somborn at the old Alexandria Hotel, where Paul Whiteman and his four-piece jazz band played. Somborn asked Bob to manage the new restaurant because he was impressed with Bob's knowledge of the restaurant business. In 1934, during the depth of the Depression, Somborn died suddenly and left the Derbies deeply in debt. Bob, who had been very close to Somborn, felt a deep loss, especially since Bob's other great friend, Mizner, had died just a few months earlier. It was Somborn's wish that Bob keep the Derbies going and also take care of his daughter from his marriage to Gloria Swanson. Bob continued the Derbies out of loyalty to Herb and concern for little Gloria; in time, he managed to pay off all the Brown Derbies' creditors and the expenses of Somborn's estate. Bob remained a kind of guardian to little Gloria. He saw to her education and, when she was married, gave her away. Little Gloria's interest in the Brown Derby became increasingly valuable as Bob, President of the Brown Derby Corporation, made the restaurants an internationally known success.

To my dear Sis — the sweetest girl in all the world Bob — 4-1?-36-

ob Cobb

Bob worked very long days when he was managing the first Brown Derby and sometimes grew weary of the familiar items on the limited menu. Late one night he prepared himself a salad of chopped leftover chicken and some other ingredients. His pals Jack Warner, Sid Grauman, Wilson Mizner, and Gene Fowler dropped by after a preview as Bob was enjoying his supper; Mizner asked what he was eating. The Foursome joined Bob and after that began ordering the "Cobb Salad." With the addition of a few ingredients, that first chopped salad evolved into the Derby's famous signature dish, though it did not appear as an official menu item until the opening of the Hollywood Brown Derby in 1929. Today, versions of the Cobb Salad are served all over the world—though there are diners and even restaurateurs who don't know how it got its name or its start—but they never have equaled the original.

Cobb Salad

SERVES 8-10

At the Brown Derby, the Cobb Salad was presented to the guests decorated as described, tossed well with the Old Fashioned French Dressing at table side and served on ice cold plates with a cold fork.

2 WHOLE CHICKEN BREASTS
1 HEAD ICEBERG LETTUCE, TRIMMED, WASHED, AND DRIED
1 HEAD ROMAINE, TRIMMED, WASHED, AND DRIED
1 BUNCH WATERCRESS
1 BUNCH CHICORY
4 TABLESPOONS CHOPPED CHIVES
4 MEDIUM TOMATOES, PEELED AND SEEDED
2 RIPE AVOCADOS
1 POUND BACON
6 HARD-BOILED EGGS
FINELY GRATED ROQUEFORT CHEESE
2 CUPS COBB'S OLD FASHIONED FRENCH DRESSING (RECIPE FOLLOWS)

Jack Warner

Sid Grauman

Wilson Mizner

Gene Fowler

Place the chicken breasts in a shallow pan or deep skillet and cover by about one inch with cold water. Bring to a simmer over medium heat, maintain the heat at a simmer, and poach the breasts for 10 to 12 minutes, depending on their size. Remove the pan from the heat and allow the chicken to cool to room temperature. When the chicken is cool, remove it from the stock (which can be strained and used for another purpose), remove and discard the skin and bones, and chop the meat finely.

Meanwhile, cook the bacon until it is crisp. Drain the bacon well and chop in roughly, by hand or in a food processor. Place the chopped bacon on paper towels and dry further, in a conventional oven on low heat or in a microwave oven, until it separates into bits. This process may need to be repeated 2 or 3 times, depending on the fat content of the bacon used.

Place the Roquefort cheese in the freezer for about 15 minutes; then remove the cheese from the freezer and grate it, using a cheese or vegetable grater.

Cut the tomatoes into small dice and sprinkle with salt and pepper.

Halve, peel, and dice the avocados; sprinkle with salt and fresh lemon juice.

Using a food processor, chop the greens finely, into $^3/_{16}$ inch bits, but do not reduce them to mush.

Finely chop the hard boiled eggs.

To assemble the salad, place all the greens in a large bowl and toss them together; spread the greens evenly in the bottom of the bowl. Arrange the bacon, egg, chicken, tomato, and cheese in strips across the greens; arrange the chopped avocado around the edge of the salad. Bring the salad to the table with the dressing alongside and toss together just before serving. Serve with Cobb's Pumpernickel Cheese Toast (recipe follows).

Note: The ingredients can be prepared several hours in advance, covered, and kept in the refrigerator; remove the ingredients about 15 minutes before assembling the salad.

Cobb's Old Fashioned French Dressing

MAKES 1 $^1/_2$ QUARTS

1 CUP WATER
1 CUP RED WINE VINEGAR
1 TEASPOON SUGAR
JUICE OF ONE LEMON
1 TABLESPOON SALT
1 TABLESPOON GROUND BLACK PEPPER
1 TABLESPOON WORCESTERSHIRE SAUCE
1 TABLESPOON DRY ENGLISH MUSTARD
1 CLOVE GARLIC, MINCED
1 CUP OLIVE OIL
3 CUPS SALAD OIL

Blend together all ingredients except the oils. Using a whisk or food processor, combine the oils and add them in a very fine stream, continuing to whisk until the mixture is well combined. Chill and shake thoroughly before serving.

Note: This dressing can be varied in numerous ways. Fresh dill, tarragon, or

rosemary can be added. This can be used as a base for Ranch, Caesar or Thousand Island dressings; it is also a marvelous marinade for vegetables, meats, or fish that are to be broiled or grilled.

Cobb's Pumpernickel Cheese Toast

This toasted delight came from Bob Cobb's desire to curb any waste in the Brown Derby Restaurants. Why not take the day old bread and make melba toast? You can use rye bread or even bagels, but pumpernickel was the favorite at the Derby.

Slicing the bread "paper thin" is the key to success. There are small electric slicers for the home that do an excellent job. It helps to partially freeze the loaf of bread so that it does not tear in the slicing.

Preheat the broiler, defrost as many slices as you want to serve (simply separate the slices and they will be at room temperature in a few minutes). Brush with a small amount of melted butter or margarine and place the slices in a single layer on a cookie sheet. Sprinkle with Parmesan cheese and toast under a hot broiler. Watch carefully, in a minute or two, when the cheese bubbles and the ends curl, the toast is done.

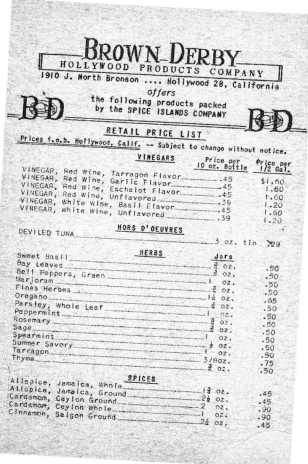

The Hollywood Brown Derby

1940S VIEW of the Hollywood Brown Derby's dining room looking toward the front doors. The signature brown leather booths were designed to be low so that people could see and be seen, and this also encouraged the table hopping that became a way of life at the Derby. The booths near the entrance and along walls were reserved for the movie and broadcasting elite. Good service was critical and the dining room was heavily staffed with waiters in starched white linen jackets.

The caricatures, beginning to fill up the walls in this photograph, began during the Depression in 1933. A young man from Poland named Eddie Vitch approached Bob Cobb and offered to sketch the Derby's famous patrons in exchange for something to eat. Bob pointed out several celebrities and with a few swift, bold brush strokes, Vitch created brilliant caricatures. Bob hired him on the spot and the drawings quickly became Hollywood's Wall of Fame. Vitch made hundreds of sketches in the next few years before returning to Europe. Famous patrons wanted to be caricatured and there was constant jockeying for position—the front wall over the entrance was considered the most important. Ambitious agents tried to have their clients' images placed alongside those of Hollywood's greats. The drawings were constantly being moved to keep up with romances and breakups or the shifting power at the studios; the prominence of the caricatures became the barometer that measured the rise and fall of Hollywood's most prominent citizens.

Interior of the Hollywood Derby

Charles "Buddy" Rogers and Mary Pickford

Mary Pickford and Buddy Rogers starred together in her last silent film, *My Best Girl*, and were married from 1937 until her death in 1979. Pickford was "America's Sweetheart" and the greatest female star of the silent era. In 1919, Pickford formed United Artists with D. W. Griffith, Charlie Chaplin and Douglas Fairbanks. She and Fairbanks, whom she married that year, became the king and queen of Hollywood and Pickfair, their estate in Beverly Hills was their palace. Her films included *Rebecca of Sunnybrook Farm* and *Coquette* (1929) her Academy Award-winning sound debut.

Buddy starred in *Wings*, a silent film which won the first Best Picture Award in 1927 and in real life was a Commander in the Naval Air force during World War II. After Mary died Buddy sold the original house and now lives on the Pickfair Estate in a new house with his wife Beverly. Buddy was from Kansas City, as was I; when I married Earl Bernheimer his father, Judge Rogers officiated.

Jean Harlow

Jean Harlow

The original platinum blonde, Harlow was discovered by twenty-three-year-old Howard Hughes for his World War I epic *Hell's Angels* in 1930. She became a star overnight. At MGM she matured as an actress and comedienne; George Cukor recognized her natural flair for comedy and put her in the all-star production *Dinner at Eight*.

Harlow had a long affair with William Powell and was still in love with him when she died of uremic poisoning. She was only twenty-six years old. For years Powell sent fresh flowers to her grave. Jean Harlow's caricature hung next to Powell's in the Hollywood Derby until he married Diana Lewis.

Spencer and Louise Tracy

The Tracys dine on French Onion Soup Brown Derby in a rare photograph. One of the greatest actors in film, Spencer Tracy won back- to- back Academy Awards for *Captains Courageous* (1937) and *Boys Town* (1938). He made nine films with Katharine Hepburn—the first was *Woman of the Year* (1942)—and their chemistry on the screen was unmistakable. Off screen their chemistry lasted for twenty- seven years and ended with Spencer's death just days after he completed work in *Guess Whose Coming to Dinner*. No picture exists of Tracy and Hepburn in the Brown Derby; their relationship was one of the most private that Hollywood has ever known. Tracy and his wife, a devout Catholic who would never divorce, were married for forty-four years.

French Onion Soup Brown Derby

SERVES 8

$^1/_4$ POUND BUTTER
2 $^1/_2$ POUNDS ONIONS, SLICED
1 QUART BEEF STOCK, HOMEMADE OR GOOD QUALITY STORE-BOUGHT
1 QUART CHICKEN STOCK, HOMEMADE OR GOOD QUALITY STORE-BOUGHT
2 TABLESPOONS WORCESTERSHIRE SAUCE
1 BAY LEAF
1 $^1/_2$ TEASPOONS CELERY SALT
1 TEASPOON BLACK PEPPER OR 12 PEPPERCORNS, CRUSHED
SALT
1 FRENCH BAGUETTE, CUT INTO 8 ($^1/_2$-INCH) SLICES
GRATED IMPORTED PARMESAN CHEESE (ABOUT $^1/_2$ CUP)

Heat butter in heavy kettle. Add sliced onions and brown well, stirring constantly. Add beef and chicken stock, Worcestershire Sauce, bay leaf, celery salt, and pepper. Simmer for 40 minutes. Salt to taste and discard the bay leaf.

Butter bread slices and sprinkle with cheese; toast the bread under broiler until browned and bubbly. Divide the soup among 8 heated individual bowls and float a piece of toast on each. Pass additional Parmesan cheese at the table.

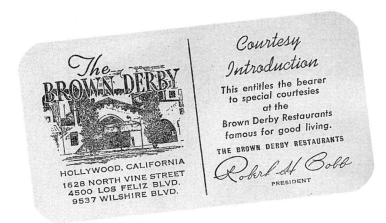

Brown Derby Double-Strength Chicken Soup with Matzo Balls

SERVES 4 TO 6

SOUP
1 WHOLE (5 POUND) ROASTING CHICKEN OR HEN
6 STALKS CELERY, TRIMMED AND WASHED
1 LEEK, TRIMMED AND WASHED CAREFULLY
6 WHOLE BLACK PEPPERCORNS
1 MEDIUM-SIZED ONION, PEELED
2 MEDIUM-SIZED DRIED BAY LEAVES
4 SPRIGS PARSLEY
SALT

Place chicken and all the ingredients except the salt in a large heavy kettle or stock pot with a close-fitting cover. Add water to cover by almost 2 inches. Bring to a low boil, lower the heat and simmer gently for $2\,^1/_2$ to 3 hours, until the chicken is very tender but does not fall from bones. Set aside to cool to room temperature. Remove the chicken, strain the broth, and discard the vegetables. Return the broth to the heat and reduce it by $^1/_3$. Reserve the chicken for another use.

MATZO BALLS
2 EGGS
1 CUP MATZO MEAL
4 TABLESPOONS CHICKEN BROTH
3 TABLESPOONS BUTTER
PINCH NUTMEG
1 TEASPOON TABLE SALT
2 TABLESPOONS CHOPPED CHIVES
1 TEASPOON BAKING POWDER

Whip eggs in bowl until foamy. Add matzo meal, chicken broth, butter, nutmeg, salt, chives, and baking powder. Mix briskly until well combined; set aside for 2 or 3 minutes. With buttered hands shape the dough into balls about the size of marbles. Bring the soup to a boil, drop in the matzo balls, lower the heat and cook for 12 minutes. Serve immediately.

(Matzo balls may be kept in a shallow pan, submerged in the broth and covered with waxed paper, in the refrigerator.)

Eddie Cantor

Ruby Keeler, Eddie Cantor, Al Jolson
Al Jolson made film history in 1927 as the star of the first talkie, *The Jazz Singer*. He was married to the dancer Ruby Keeler who starred with Dick Powell in seven Warner Brothers musicals in the 1930s. Many of their classics—*Gold Diggers of 1933* and *42nd Street* among them—featured the innovative and elaborate choreography of Busby Berkeley. Eddie Cantor, who was a star first in the Ziegfeld Follies, went on to a big career in films and a very popular radio show.

Wallace Beery

Bert Wheeler, Wallace Beery, Tom Mix, Robert Woolsey, Carol Ann Beery

Marlene Dietrich, known for her masculine attire onscreen and off, shocked Hollywood and made headlines in 1933 by appearing at the Hollywood Brown Derby in slacks. Marlene was shocked in turn when Bob refused to let her into the derby. At that the comic team of Wheeler and Woolsey left the restaurant and returned wearing skirts, Wheeler still smoking his cigar. They were joined by Tom Mix and Wallace Beery and Beery's daughter Carol Ann. It was thirty-five years before Bob finally lifted the ban. The press credited my preference for pant suits, but in truth Bob knew that the times had changed.

Marlene Dietrich

*M*arlene Dietrich and Eric Maria Remarque
Dietrich, wearing a chic suit, dined with the famed
German writer Eric Maria Remarque in the Beverly
Hills Brown Derby. They resumed their romance,
which began in Europe, when they were reunited
in California in 1939—with neighboring bungalows
at the Beverly Hills Hotel. Unconventional Marlene
also arranged a room for her daughter and a suite
for her husband, Rudi Sieber (whom she never
divorced) in the main hotel; there even was a room
down the hall for Rudi's mistress. Dietrich had
returned to film *Destry Rides Again*, which became
the vehicle for one of Hollywood's most spectacular comebacks.

    All Quiet on the Western Front had made
Remarque the bestselling author of the twentieth
century at the time. The brilliant film version of the
anti-war novel established his reputation in
Hollywood in 1930. That was also the year that
Marlene became an international star in *The Blue
Angel*, her first film with director Josef von
Sternberg. Her collaborations with Sternberg were
among the greatest in film history.

Bob Cobb and Tom Mix

Mix, the most famous of all the silent movie cowboys, and Tony the Wonder Horse thrilled audiences with breathtaking stunts in dozens of westerns in the twenties. Tom was a great friend of Bob's and a frequent guest at the Brown Derby—Tony even had a hitching post outside the Hollywood Derby. Always a showman, Tom is sporting a derby while Bob wears the cowboy hero's signature white Stetson.

Bob was the last person to hear from his old friend before Tom's fatal car accident in 1940. Tom was returning to Los Angeles in his custom-made convertible Cord Phaeton when he sent a telegram to Bob: "Coming home—meet you at the Derby for dinner."

Tom Mix

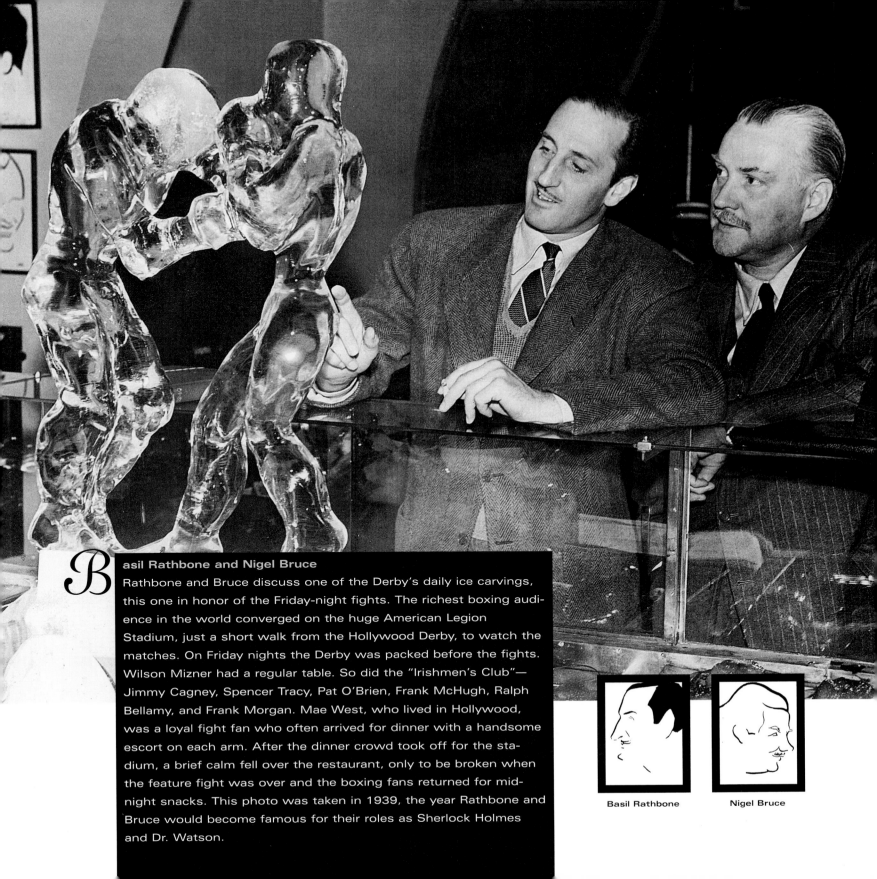

*B*asil Rathbone and Nigel Bruce

Rathbone and Bruce discuss one of the Derby's daily ice carvings, this one in honor of the Friday-night fights. The richest boxing audience in the world converged on the huge American Legion Stadium, just a short walk from the Hollywood Derby, to watch the matches. On Friday nights the Derby was packed before the fights. Wilson Mizner had a regular table. So did the "Irishmen's Club"— Jimmy Cagney, Spencer Tracy, Pat O'Brien, Frank McHugh, Ralph Bellamy, and Frank Morgan. Mae West, who lived in Hollywood, was a loyal fight fan who often arrived for dinner with a handsome escort on each arm. After the dinner crowd took off for the stadium, a brief calm fell over the restaurant, only to be broken when the feature fight was over and the boxing fans returned for midnight snacks. This photo was taken in 1939, the year Rathbone and Bruce would become famous for their roles as Sherlock Holmes and Dr. Watson.

Basil Rathbone   Nigel Bruce

Brown Derby Grapefruit Cake

Louella, who loved desserts, dieted constantly. After one of her weekly staff meetings in the Derby's American Room, she informed Bob that she was not coming back if he didn't come up with a nonfattening dessert. Bob's idea to "put grapefruit on something, because everyone knows it's slimming" was the origin of the Brown Derby's classic Grapefruit Cake.

$2^{1}/_{4}$ CUPS SIFTED CAKE FLOUR

$1^{1}/_{2}$ CUPS SUGAR

3 TEASPOONS BAKING POWDER

1 TEASPOON SALT

5 EGG YOLKS

$^{1}/_{2}$ CUP CORN OIL

$^{3}/_{4}$ CUP COLD WATER

ZEST OF 1 LEMON

2 TEASPOONS VANILLA EXTRACT

8 EGG WHITES

$^{1}/_{2}$ TEASPOON CREAM OF TARTAR

BROWN DERBY GRAPEFRUIT

FROSTING (RECIPE FOLLOWS)

Preheat oven to 325° F. Sift together the flour, sugar, baking powder, and salt in a large mixing bowl. Make a well in the middle of these ingredients and add, one at a time, egg yolks, oil, water, lemon zest and vanilla. Blend with wooden spoon until smooth.

Whip the egg whites with the cream of tartar until very stiff peaks form. Gently fold the egg yolk mixture into egg whites until just blended. Do not stir this mixture. Pour the batter into two 10-inch round ungreased cake pans and bake in the oven for 55 minutes; increase the temperature to 350° F and bake for an additional 10 minutes. The cake is done when top springs back to the touch.

Invert the cake pans on a rack to cool. Prop them up if necessary so that the air can circulate between the layers and the tabletop. When cool, loosen sides and remove cake layers. Place 1 layer bottom side up on serving plate. Spread with frosting and top with grapefruit sections. Cover with second layer, bottom side down, and frost top and sides. Garnish with grapefruit sections.

Brown Derby Grapefruit Frosting

1 (2-POUND) CAN GRAPEFRUIT SECTIONS, WELL DRAINED
1 CUP POWDERED SUGAR
24 OUNCES CREAM CHEESE, SOFTENED
12 DROPS YELLOW FOOD COLORING
4 TEASPOONS LEMON JUICE
2 TEASPOONS GRATED LEMON RIND

Mash 6 grapefruit sections with a fork into small bits. Beat cheese with lemon juice until fluffy. Gradually beat in sugar and blend well. Add coloring, lemon rind, and 4 teaspoons of crushed grapefruit sections.

Louella Parsons

Louella Parsons with the composer and lyricist Jerome Kern

Louella's Hollywood column began in 1925 and ran for decades in the Hearst newspapers. Her rivalry with Hedda Hopper was real, and I always gave them equal access to any information I might have. Louella wrote from her home on Maple Drive in Beverly Hills and usually had lunch at her reserved booth in her unofficial office: the Hollywood Brown Derby. Louella's cousin, Margaret "Maggie" Ettinger, was in public relations. The Brown Derby was her client from the day it opened and Maggie had her offices upstairs, over the restaurant.

Hedda Hopper

oseph Cotton, Hedda Hopper, Orson Welles

Welles and Cotton were joined by Hedda Hopper at the Brown Derby in Hollywood. Welles was just twenty-five years old when he arrived in Hollywood in 1940 to produce, direct, coauthor (with Herman J. Mankiewicz) and act in his stunning film debut, *Citizen Kane*. Cotton starred along with Welles and Ruth Warrick in what is considered by many to be the greatest film ever made. Welles followed that artistic triumph with *The Magnificent Ambersons*, also starring Joseph Cotton, in 1942.

The enormous controversy surrounding *Citizen Kane* was due to its obvious reference to newspaper tycoon William Randolph Hearst and Hearst's relationship with Marion Davies. Louella Parsons, who was employed by the Hearst newspapers, used her influence to defend Hearst and damaged the box office returns of *Citizen Kane* in spite of its critical acclaim. Louella and her rival gossip columnist, Hedda Hopper, had enormous power through their combined audience of 75 million readers. Hedda initially complained that the film's photography was old-fashioned and the writing corny, but by the time this photograph was taken in 1943 she was a Welles supporter.

Darryl Zanuck **Joseph Schenck** **Harry Cohn**

*O*arryl and Virginia Zanuck

Zanuck's first job at Warner Brothers was writing scripts for the great dog star Rin-Tin-Tin in 1924. Three years later he was vice president in charge of production. After a disagreement in 1933, he offered to resign. Zanuck and his wife, Virginia, were at the Hollywood Brown Derby when he interrupted his lunch to meet with the Warners again; he was surprised when they accepted his resignation. The news flew around the town quickly and within twenty minutes of his return to the Derby, the incoming phone lines were busy with offers for Zanuck.

Zanuck's partnership with Joseph Schenck, the president of United Artists, was the genesis of 20th Century Films. In 1935 20th Century merged with Fox Film Corporation to become 20th Century-Fox, and for the next twenty years Zanuck headed the studio. He told Hedda Hopper, "Out here, if you make a bad picture it's very doubtful that you'll get a good table at the Brown Derby," but in any case the front booth was reserved for studio heads Zanuck, Schenck, the Warner brothers, and Harry Cohn.

Errol Flynn

Errol Flynn and Buddy Ernst

During a meeting at the Derby, Errol Flynn used a napkin to make a point with his friend Buddy Ernst.

In 1941, I was staying in Los Angeles with William and Brownie Wilkerson waiting for my divorce to become final. Billy owned the *Hollywood Reporter* and had just opened Ciro's, which would become a legendary Hollywood nightclub. My attorney, Jerry Giesler, had told me not to go out until my divorce was granted, so I assumed that I wouldn't attend Brownie and Billy's big New Year's Eve party at Ciro's. But the divorce decree came through two days before New Year's Eve. Billy then asked me who, in all of Hollywood, I would like spend New Year's Eve with. That was an almost bewildering offer for a newcomer from Kansas City. Like so many women I had thought Errol Flynn incredibly handsome in *The Adventures of Robin Hood*, so I chose Errol. The great designer Howard Greer (who did Katharine Hepburn's costumes in *Bringing Up Baby*) created a divine dress for me in just two days. Errol was mobbed and women went wild when we entered the club. That party was extraordinary. The guests included Darryl and Virginia Zanuck, Betty Grable and George Raft, Rita Hayworth and her first husband, Ed Judson, and Marlene Dietrich with Jean Gabin. The next day Errol invited me out on his yacht, *the Sirocco*. Also on board was Jane Stoneham. Jane, whose half brother, Horace Stoneham, owned the New York Giants, later married Freeman Gosden (Amos of "Amos 'n' Andy").

Charles Boyer

Charles Boyer and Ingrid Bergman

The stars of *Gaslight* (1944), dining at the Hollywood Derby in 1948. Bergman won the Oscar for her portrayal of a woman whose husband was trying to drive her crazy. That performance, along with other successes like *Casablanca* with Humphrey Bogart and *The Bells of Saint Mary's* with Bing Crosby, made the fresh-faced Swedish actress one of the industry's biggest stars.

But in 1949 the press reported her romance with director Roberto Rossellini when she was appearing on the screen as Joan of Arc. This was during filming in Italy, and it was a sensational scandal when Bergman abandoned her husband, Peter Lindstrom, and her young daughter, Pia, to remain with Rossellini. Bergman was denounced by the American press when she gave birth to Rossellini's son, Robertino, in 1950, though the couple married shortly thereafter. Their twins, Ingrid and Isabella (now an actress) were born in 1952. In one of Hollywood's greatest comebacks, Bergman made *Anastasia* (1956) in London and returned to the United States for the first time in eight years to claim her second Academy Award.

*O*liver Hardy and Stan Laurel
The timeless and universal humor
of Laurel and Hardy made them
the best-loved comedy team in
the movies. Laurel and Hardy first
wore the derbies that became
their trademark in a 1927 silent
comedy short. Here they are
seated beneath one of the
Hollywood Brown Derby's trademark copper light fixtures. The
year is 1940, when Laurel and
Hardy made their last picture for
Hal Roach. Their association with
Roach had produced their greatest films, including the Academy
Award-winning short *The Music
Box* and *Sons of the Desert*.

Myrna Loy and David O. Selznick

The legendary producer David O. Selznick and lovely Myrna Loy dined together at the Brown Derby. Loy's extraordinary career spanned seven decades and more than one hundred movies, including *The Best Years of Our Lives*, her favorite role. She was voted "Queen of Hollywood" in the 1938 popularity poll that also proclaimed Clark Gable "King." Gable's title was forever secure after his performance as Rhett Butler in Selznick's triumph, *Gone with the Wind*. The Civil War epic was produced through Selznick's independent production company, Selznick International Pictures. A perfectionist known for his meticulous attention to every detail of a production, Selznick's classics include *Intermezzo* and *Rebecca*.

ill Chilias

As maitre d' at the Hollywood Brown Derby from 1929 to 1955, Bill Chilias was known by all—being known by him was a sign of status in Hollywood. The demand for tables often exceeded the supply but he handled all situations diplomatically. Reservations were mandatory and the most desired booths were held for the best known or most regular customers. The importance of being known by Chilias and getting a good table at the Derby was demonstrated when his Christmas tips exceeded $10,000 in the late thirties. When one's table was ready, Chilias would part with a flourish the red velvet rope that divided the foyer from the dining room.

irginia Mayo and Gus Constance

Maitre d' Gus Constance seems to enjoy being served by the lovely actress Virginia Mayo. Virginia lost a bet to Gus, and as a result, she waited on him in the famous starched bell-skirt uniform that Brown Derby waitresses had been wearing for twenty years. As Virginia demonstrated, the uniform charmingly tipped up in back when the waitresses leaned over. The waitresses were so pretty that half of them were hired by studios within a month of the opening of the Beverly Derby.

enny Massi

Waiter and bartender to the stars, Massi was a well-known and much loved fixture at the Derby for forty-six years. Benny was at the Derby from the opening day of "The Hat" in 1926 (he served Valentino before his death that same year). When the Bamboo Room opened in 1936, Benny was on hand to mix his perfect martinis and the new specialty, the Bamboo, which was made with rum and limes. He was the personal favorite of many stars, including Louella Parsons and Bing Crosby, for whom the Brown Derby catered parties at their homes. Knowing that Benny was also Dorothy Lamour's favorite, Bob Cobb selected him to deliver and serve dinner to Dorothy, complete with Brown Derby service, each night during a hospital stay.

Humphrey and Mayo Bogart

The press labeled them "The Battling Bogarts" for their heavy drinking and public arguments, which were legendary. Bogart and actress Mayo Methot—he nicknamed her Sluggy—were married on August 20, 1938. They had worked together with Bette Davis in *Marked Woman* and lived together while Bogey was still married to Mary Philips. Bogart and Mayo divorced in 1945 after Bogart's affair with his nineteen-year-old costar in *To Have and Have Not* became public. The nineteen-year-old was Lauren Bacall, who became Bogart's wife and remained so until his death from lung cancer in 1957.

W. C. Fields

Notorious for his dislike of children, Fields was mobbed by his young fans in front of the Hollywood Derby. Fields was a Derby regular from the beginning, often in the company of two of the greatest wits of the day, Will Rogers and Wilson Mizner. Fields, the star of *My Little Chickadee* and *Never Give a Sucker an Even Break*, had started his career as a professional juggler. One evening, Fanny Brice was with Fields at the Derby when he threw his waiter's watch, his cigar, and a basket of dinner rolls into the air and juggled them expertly.

Autograph seekers showed up ritually outside the Hollywood Derby especially at lunch. Walter Winchell was familiar with the routine because he reported from the Derby when he was on the West Coast. Winchell's tip to his readers hoping to see movie stars was that they should visit the Brown Derby. He warned, however, against bothering celebrities inside the restaurant. That, he reported, was "the shortcut to banishment."

Walter Winchell   W.C. Fields

Cary Grant and Mrs. Ray Milland

Grant's famous profile was a familiar sight in the Brown Derby, both in caricature and in person. He was one of Hollywood's legendary leading men and epitomized the term movie star. He was born into poverty and created an image that was the same in person as it was on film. He once said, "I pretended to be a certain kind of man on screen . . . and I became that man in life. I became me."

Cary Grant's caricature was drawn by Zel, the Derby's second caricaturist. We never knew him by any other name. The caricatures were created with a few quick strokes while the celebrity was at the Derby. When the drawings were completed, they were autographed by the subject, which is just what Cary Grant has done here.

Cary Grant

arbara Hutton and Bruce Cabot

Hutton became one of the world's richest women when she inherited the Woolworth fortune at the age of five. Here she is dining with actor Bruce Cabot. At the time, Hutton was married to Cary Grant, who became her third husband in 1942. The press often referred to the couple as "Cash and Cary" during their brief and highly publicized marriage.

In the 1930s, the Hollywood Brown Derby became the first restaurant to offer telephones, delivered upon request, to tables. Calls received at the Derby's switchboard were relayed by loudspeaker and the customer was paged. To some, the number of times one was paged was an indication of power and importance. Some people, agents and advertising men in particular, arranged to be paged at the Derby.

Caramel Custard

SERVES 8

Hutton's favorite was the caramel custard that was brought to the table in its ceramic custard cup and then inverted onto the dessert plate. When the cup was removed, the silky custard and its delicious caramel sauce were revealed.

$2\,^1/_3$ CUPS SUGAR
1 QUART MILK
8 WHOLE EGGS
$^1/_2$ VANILLA BEAN
PINCH OF SALT

Pour $1\,^1/_3$ cups of sugar into a heavy pan and heat over medium-high heat, shaking the pan from time to time, but not stirring, until sugar has liquified. The sugar should melt into a light golden brown syrup. Butter the sides of 8 4-ounce custard cups. Pour the caramel sauce into the cups about $^1/_2$ inch deep; set aside.

Bring the milk to a boil. Mix together the eggs, remaining 1 cup sugar, vanilla, and salt. Slowly pour half the milk into the egg mixture, stirring constantly, then pour the mixture back into the remaining milk. Stir over low heat until the mixture thickens slightly; do not let the mixture come close to a boil, or it will curdle. Pour the custard into the cups and place them in a pan of hot water; bake 15 to 20 minutes or until a cake tester inserted into the center of the custards comes out clean. Baking times will vary with the thickness of the custard cups used.

𝓑ob Cobb, Gail Patrick, Marian Marsh, Howard Hughes
Eccentric Howard Hughes was a handsome young million-
aire in 1936, when he and actress Marian Marsh enjoyed
a formal evening with Bob Cobb and Gail Patrick. Bob and
Gail had married earlier that year and remained friends
after their divorce three years later. When Hughes came
into the Hollywood Brown Derby he insisted on the privacy of one of the booths at the back of the restaurant.
Hughes's career in Hollywood spanned his productions of
Hell's Angels (1930) and *The Outlaw* (1943) and a control-
ling interest in RKO (1948–1957). When he set a speed
record with his flight around the world, Hughes became
an international figure, but his airplane crash in Beverly
Hills left him facially scarred and increasingly reclusive.

Millicent Hearst with her family
William Randolph Hearst met his wife, Millicent, when she was a sixteen-year-old dancer on Broadway. Their five sons were George, William Randolph, Jr., John, Randolph, and David. Here, Mrs. Hearst, David, his wife Hope, and William Randolph, Jr., enjoy a traditional roast turkey dinner at the Beverly Hills Brown Derby.

Marion Davies, Gene Raymond, Bob Cobb
Bob, on the arm of his old friend Marion Davies, chatted with Gene Raymond in the American Room of the Hollywood Brown Derby in 1939. Marion's affair with William Randolph Hearst had been public for twenty years and would continue until his death in 1951.

William Randolph Hearst

Marion Davies

Roasted Stuffed Turkey with Giblet Gravy

SERVES 10 TO 12 PLUS LEFTOVERS

18- TO 20-POUND OVEN-READY HEN TURKEY
SALT AND PEPPER
$2^1/_2$ QUARTS BROWN DERBY DRESSING (RECIPE FOLLOWS)
3 CARROTS, DICED
2 ONIONS, DICED
2 STALKS CELERY, DICED
$1^1/_2$ CUPS ALL-PURPOSE FLOUR
$1^1/_2$ QUARTS HOMEMADE OR GOOD-QUALITY STORE-BOUGHT CHICKEN STOCK

Preheat oven to 350°F. Remove the giblets and neck from the turkey cavity and wash and dry the turkey well. Season the turkey well with salt and pepper inside and out. Stuff the neck and body cavities with dressing and tie securely. Place the bird in a roasting pan and brush it generously with melted butter. Make a tent with heavy-duty aluminum foil and cover the turkey completely with it. Roast the turkey for 20 minutes per pound, basting frequently.

While turkey is in the oven cook giblets and chop them very finely.

About 1 hour before turkey is done, remove the foil tent and add the carrots, onions, and celery to roasting pan. When the turkey is done, remove it from the pan and cover it with foil to keep warm. Remove the vegetables with a slotted spoon and reserve them. Let the pan drippings settle and skim the fat. Heat the drippings over medium heat and add flour, a little at a time, blending and browning well. Add the chicken stock and vegetables, blending well, and simmer for 20 minutes. Strain the gravy through a fine sieve and add giblets; serve with the turkey.

Brown Derby Turkey Dressing

MAKES 2 QUARTS

2 LARGE LOAVES SOURDOUGH FRENCH BREAD
$^3/_4$ TO 1 CUP BUTTER, MELTED
2 POUNDS GROUND SAUSAGE
3 LARGE ONIONS, DICED
2 CELERY HEARTS, DICED
2 TART APPLES, PEELED, CORED, AND THINLY SLICED
2 POUNDS ROASTED CHESTNUTS OR 2 CANS SLICED WATER CHESTNUTS, DRAINED
FRESH CHOPPED PARSLEY TO TASTE
1 TO 2 TABLESPOONS DRIED SAGE
2 TEASPOONS CELERY SALT
2 TEASPOONS NUTMEG
SALT AND PEPPER TO TASTE
EVAPORATED MILK

Preheat the oven to 350° F. Cut French bread into small cubes. Toss cubes with the melted butter, spread in a single layer on cookie sheets, and bake, tossing occasionally, until golden brown; place in a large bowl.

Crumble sausage into a frying pan and cook thoroughly over medium heat. Drain, reserving fat, and add cooked sausage to the croutons. Sauté the onions and celery in the sausage drippings over medium heat until opaque but not brown, about 10 to 15 minutes. Remove with a slotted spoon and add to the croutons and sausage. Add the next 7 ingredients and toss thoroughly. Use evaporated milk to moisten dressing to desired consistency (it will not alter the flavor of the dressing).

Brown Derby catering trucks

The Bamboo Room

The Bamboo Room was the Hollywood Brown Derby's first cocktail lounge. When the Derby opened in 1929, Prohibition was the law and was not repealed for four more years. In 1933 a service bar was installed at the back of the dining room; waiters also wheeled a cocktail cart from booth to booth and prepared drinks for customers at their tables.

February 6, 1936: Carole Lombard was the host of a glamorous evening that officially opened the room. Tropical palms, bamboo chairs covered with zebra prints, and a sandlike floor gave the Bamboo Room the exotic feeling of the South Seas. Hollywood's tropical fantasies began with the opening of the Coconut Grove (decorated with hundres of prop palm trees from *The Sheik*) at the Ambassador Hotel in 1921, and was played out in numerous restaurants and nightclubs, including the Seven Seas, the Tropics, Don the Beachcomber, and the Hawaiian Paradise, through the 1930s.

Janet Gaynor and Tyrone Power
In 1931, Tyrone Power, then seventeen, was first brought to the Brown Derby by his father, actor Tyrone Power, Sr. The Derby became a lifelong habit. Power was often there with his first wife, Annabella, and later, when he was married to Linda Christian. In the late 1930s, when Tyrone and Janet Gaynor were photographed leaving the Bamboo Room, he was a top star at Twentieth Century-Fox. Janet Gaynor, who won the first Oscar as Best Actress in *Seventh Heaven*, had been nominated for her second Academy Award for her performance in *A Star Is Born*. The David O. Selznick film about Hollywood featured the Vine Street Brown Derby.

Gail Patrick, Randolph Scott, Carole Lombard
Dark-haired beauty Gail Patrick and gorgeous
blonde Carole Lombard were cast as rival sisters in the 1936 screwball comedy *My Man
Godfrey*. Here they posed with Randy Scott.
Lombard proved herself to be one on the
screen's finest comediennes with her brilliant
performances in *Twentieth Century* and
Nothing Sacred.

Three years earlier, Gail was a
University of Alabama graduate who won the
nationwide "Panther Girl" beauty contest and
a trip to Hollywood. Gail's first husband was
Bob Cobb; they were married for three years.
Later, in the 1950s, Gail was executive producer of the Perry Mason series and married
to agent Cornwall Jackson.

*O*avid Niven, Merle Oberon, Charles Boyer and his wife, Pat Paterson

Hollywood's European community was represented that night by Charles and Pat Boyer, Merle Oberon and the British newcomer David Niven. Others were Lord and Lady Cavendish (Fred Astaire's sister, Adele). David Niven had just finished *The Charge of the Light Brigade* and was romantically linked with Merle Oberon. Born in poverty in Bombay, of a British father and an Indian mother, Oberon's real name was Queenie O'Brien. It was Alexander Korda, a Hungarian who was the most important man in the British film industry, who changed her name to Merle Oberon, changed her birthplace to Tasmania, and invented a suitable background for his new star. In time he also married her.

Charles Boyer and David Niven worked together twenty years later when Niven starred in Mike Todd's epic *Around the World in 80 Days*. During his long career as a romantic leading man, Charles Boyer was paired with many of Hollywood's most glamorous female stars, including screen goddesses Greta Garbo and Marlene Dietrich. In real life he was married to the British actress Pat Paterson from 1936 until she died of cancer in 1978 and

R

obert Taylor, Irene Hervey, Carole Lombard, Cesar Romero

Robert Taylor, who was about to become one of MGM's biggest stars, was out with actress Irene Hervey. They were an item for a couple of years before Taylor married Barbara Stanwyck. Taylor filmed *Camille* with the great Garbo later that year, while Cesar Romero played opposite Carole Lombard in *Love Before Breakfast*.

Cesar, who was a good friend of mine, grew more handsome and distinguished through the next five decades. After Bob died, Cesar became my favorite dancing partner. Many of the parties that he and I attended were held at the Beverly Wilshire Hotel and we usually finished those evenings by walking across the street to the Beverly Hills Brown Derby for a late light supper.

Newlyweds Ann and Jack Warner (right) with producer Harry Joe Brown and his wife, actress Sally Eilers

Jack and his brothers, Harry, Albert, and Sam, were movie pioneers who founded Warner Brothers studio. During Jack's reign as head of the studio, Warner Brothers ushered in the age of talking pictures with *The Jazz Singer*. He was head of production during the heady decades in which the studio produced great films that ranged from gangster pictures and musicals to classics like *Casablanca* and *My Fair Lady*. Ann and Jack Warner were Hollywood's greatest host and hostess during Hollywood's golden years. The lavish parties at their magnificent estate in Beverly Hills were without equal.

William Powell

Myrna Loy

William Powell and his wife, Diana "Mousie" Lewis, and Myrna Loy Suave William Powell and the movies' perfect wife, Myrna Loy, with his real-life wife of forty-four years, "Mousie". Powell and Loy, MGM's most popular screen couple through the 1930s, made fourteen movies together, including their most popular pairings as the sophisticated sleuths Nick and Nora Charles in The Thin Man series.

Ken Murray

**Edgar Bergen and
Charlie McCarthy**

ℰdgar Bergen with Charlie McCarthy and ken Murray
Bergen and Ken Murray are enjoying their martinis in the
Bamboo Room, but Charlie McCarthy doesn't look too
pleased with his glass of milk. Edgar Bergen and Charlie
McCarthy's guest appearance on Rudy Vallee's radio
show was the beginning of their great success. By 1938,
their Sunday evening show was number one in the rat-
ings. Ken Murray was best known for his variety revue,
Ken Murray's Blackouts, which ran for years in
Hollywood.

Jack Benny remembered having lunch with Edgar
Bergen at the Derby. Jack recalled that when he
requested the check, the waiter reacted in the silly way
Benny had come to expect. The waiter said, "Mr. Benny,
I'm surprised to hear you ask for the check." "So am I,"
Jack replied. "And that's the last time I'll ever eat lunch
with a ventriloquist."

The American Room

The private entrances at the back of the Hollywood Brown Derby allowed the stars discreet access to the American Room. The parking valets knew the celebrities' cars and didn't use claim checks. Clark Gable and Carole Lombard once left the American Room when a new attendant was on duty. "What kind of car, Mr. Gable?" the valet asked. Carole turned to Clark and said, "When they don't know your car at this place, you know you're slipping and that your next option may not be taken up."

The American Room was actually two rooms, a living room and a dining room, with sliding doors between. When both rooms were reserved, they allowed for very gracious entertaining. After a cocktail party in the living room, the sliding doors would be opened and guests would be seated in the dining room.

The American Room

To accommodate the demand for private parties, the Hollywood Brown Derby opened the American Room in 1938. Hollywood found it the perfect place to give luncheon, cocktail, and dinner parties. The room was warmly decorated with Early American antiques and the celebrities entertained in privacy—although the press was frequently invited for publicity purposes. The American Room was the setting for countless events over the years, many of which were reported in newspaper columns or magazines. Many other gatherings were truly private—family and friends celebrating birthdays, engagements, or anniversaries.

Brown Derby Special Sandwiches with Cole Slaw

Brown Derby Sandwiches were made special by the restaurant's cole slaw, which in turn was distinguished by the house Thousand Island Dressing. Some of the favorite combinations—usually made on Russian rye bread—were ham or tongue with Swiss cheese; turkey and ham; or turkey, ham, and Swiss. About 2 tablespoons of cole slaw were evenly spread over the fillings, then the sandwiches were cut crosswise into three sections and served with kosher dill pickles.

Brown Derby Cole Slaw

4 CUPS SHREDDED WHITE CABBAGE
1 CUP THOUSAND ISLAND DRESSING (RECIPE FOLLOWS)

Mix the ingredients together thoroughly and refrigerate for at least 2 hours.

Thousand Island Dressing

MAKES 1 PINT

1 $^1/_2$ CUPS BROWN DERBY MAYONNAISE (PAGE 59)
$^1/_2$ CUP BOTTLED CHILI SAUCE
$^1/_2$ LARGE GREEN BELL PEPPER, SEEDED
AND FINELY CHOPPED
$^1/_4$ CUP FINELY CHOPPED PIMIENTO
2 TABLESPOONS FINELY CHOPPED CHIVES
$^1/_4$ CUP FINELY CHOPPED CAPERS
3 HARD-BOILED EGGS, FINELY CHOPPED
1 TABLESPOON LEMON JUICE

Blend all ingredients together thoroughly and refrigerate.

usan Hayward, Joy Hodges, Rita Hayworth, Robert Stack

They were all at the beginning of their careers and no one was over twenty-one when Robert Stack, Susan Hayward, and Rita Hayworth attended a luncheon in the American Room in 1939. It was the year that Rita Hayworth made her first important film appearance in *Only Angels Have Wings*, Susan Hayward made *Beau Geste* with Gary Cooper, and Robert Stack made his screen debut in *First Love*.

      In fact, Rita Hayworth had not yet been transformed from Margarita Carmen Cansino, the daughter of a Spanish dancer, when this shot was taken. She was undergoing electrolysis treatments to accentuate her widow's peak and raise her hairline at the temples. Soon her hair would be lightened from brunette to auburn to complete the metamorphosis.

      Like scores of other actresses, Susan Hayward came to Hollywood in 1937 to test for *Gone with the Wind*. Hayward reached the peak of her career two decades later, when she won the Academy Award for *I Want to Live!* in 1958.

      Throughout his career, Robert Stack was often surrounded by beautiful women. Perhaps his best role was in *Written on the Wind* (1956), with Dorothy Malone and Lauren Bacall. Ida Lupino was — and is — one of the few women to cross over from acting to directing or producing.

Brown Derby Mayonnaise

MAKES 1 PINT

3 EGG YOLKS
1 TABLESPOON MILD VINEGAR
1 TEASPOON SALT
$1^1/_2$ CUPS SALAD OIL
$^1/_2$ TEASPOON DRY MUSTARD
JUICE OF $^1/_2$ LEMON
$^1/_2$ TEASPOON WORCESTERSHIRE SAUCE

In a food processor, beat the egg yolks until they thicken and are pale yellow in color. Add the salt, mustard and $^1/_2$ tablespoon vinegar and combine well. Add the oil by drops until the yolk mixture begins to pull together and thicken, then add in a fine stream. All the oil should be incorporated into the egg mixture. Once a mayonnaise has been achieved, add the remaining vinegar and lemon juice. Mix in 1 tablespoon of boiling water and store, tightly covered, in the refrigerator.

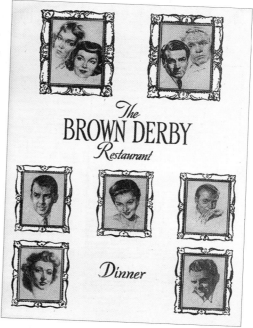

*B*ob Cobb, George Jessel, Fred Haney

Baseball fans Bob Cobb and George Jessel are getting batting hints — with the aid of Jessel's cigar — from a real pro, Fred Haney. Fred managed the Milwaukee Braves when they won the pennant in the 1957 World Series against the New York Yankees. Fred had earlier managed Bob Cobb's Hollywood Stars and was the first general manager of Gene Autry's California Angels in 1960.

Bette Davis

Davis was the guest of honor In the American Room at a luncheon given by the Hollywood Women's Press Club. She had just won the 1938 Best Actress Award (her second) for her performance in William Wyler's *Jezebel*. Bette was nominated for the next four years. Later, she claimed to have named the Oscar statuette after her first husband, Harmon Oscar Nelson, when she noticed that from behind, it resembled him.

*G*eorge Burns and Gracie Allen with William S. Paley, in the American Room
William S. Paley, president of CBS, personified the power and glamour of
what became, under his leadership, the most powerful communications
company in the world. In 1938, CBS built the Columbia Square broadcasting
studios at Sunset and Gower. The studio was just around the corner from the
Hollywood Brown Derby, which became the place where the radio performers, writers, and directors gathered. When Paley was in Los Angeles he also
came to the Derby. This photograph was taken at a private party in the
American Room that he gave for George Burns and Gracie Allen in 1943.

Paley's talent searches in the early days of radio recruited relatively
unknown performers, including Bing Crosby, Kate Smith, and the Mills
Brothers. Paley's trademark was programming that mixed mass entertainment, high culture, and news gathering that set the standard for broadcast
journalism. The network took its pioneering role in radio to the new medium
of television. Early CBS-TV hits included "I Love Lucy," "Playhouse 90," and
"CBS Reports." Burns and Allen had their TV premiere on CBS in 1950.

Paley's personal life also made news, especially when he married the
dazzling Barbara Cushing Mortimer. Universally known as "Babe," she was
considered one of the most beautiful and best dressed women in the world.

Cheese Soufflé

SERVES 4

The Brown Derby chefs frequently prepared this classic cheese soufflé for Gracie Allen on the afternoon of her broadcasts and liked to think that it had a little bit to do with her unique style of light comedy.

$^1/_2$ CUP WATER
3 TABLESPOONS ALL-PURPOSE FLOUR
$^1/_4$ CUP BUTTER
4 WHOLE EGGS
SALT TO TASTE
1 $^1/_4$ CUPS FRESHLY GRATED PARMESAN CHEESE
DASH NUTMEG
6 EGG WHITES

Preheat the oven to 425° F. Butter and flour a 2 quart soufflé dish with 3 $^1/_2$ inch sides. Combine water, butter, salt, and nutmeg in a heavy saucepan and boil until butter is melted. Add flour to the boiling mixture. Continue mixing vigorously with wooden spoon until the mixture forms a ball. Over low heat, add the eggs one at a time, beating vigorously to blend into a smooth paste before adding next egg. After all the eggs have been incorporated, add the cheese and mix again. After the cheese has been thoroughly blended into the mixture, remove the pan from the heat. Beat the egg whites until stiff and fold them into the mixture. Gently pour the mixture into the prepared pan. Set the soufflé dish in a larger pan of hot water and place it in the oven for about 35 minutes. When the soufflé has risen and is a light golden brown, serve it immediately.

For Good Living

Cordially
Yours

The Brown Derby

Romance

Clark Gable and Carole Lombard

Gable and Lombard were the most glamorous and romantic couple ever. Clark proposed to Carole in booth number five in the Hollywood Derby without realizing he was under the watchful eye of the caricature of Carole's first husband, William Powell (far right). Clark carefully worked out this menu in advance with Bob Cobb. That evening, the staff was alerted to make certain that everything was perfect for Hollywood's biggest romance.

Clark Gable   **Carole Lombard**

Old-Fashioned Pot Roast Brown Derby

TUESDAY'S SPECIALTY OF THE DAY — SERVES 6 TO 8

Their engagement dinner was elegant, but Carole and Clark really preferred the Brown Derby's simple foods. On their rare nights out, they were regularly at the Derby, and their favorite dinner was our Old-Fashioned Pot Roast and Potato Pancakes. Gary Cooper and Betty Grable loved this dish, too.

1 (8-POUND) ROLLED AND TIED CHUCK ROAST
SALT AND PEPPER
$\frac{1}{3}$ CUP OIL
1 MEDIUM ONION, SLICED
3 MEDIUM CARROTS, DICED
2 STALKS CELERY, TRIMMED AND DICED
1 LEEK, WASHED, TRIMMED, AND DICED
$\frac{1}{2}$ CUP ALL-PURPOSE FLOUR
2 CUPS BURGUNDY WINE
$\frac{1}{4}$ TEASPOON DRIED BASIL
1 DRIED BAY LEAF
3 FRESH TOMATOES, DICED
$2\frac{1}{2}$ CUPS TOMATO PURÉE
2 CLOVES GARLIC
1 TABLESPOON PAPRIKA
1 TABLESPOON CELERY SALT
$1\frac{1}{2}$ QUARTS BEEF STOCK, HOMEMADE OR GOOD-QUALITY STORE-BOUGHT

Seafood Derby Cocktail

French Onion Soup

Tournedos of Beef Filet, Derby House
Saffron Rice
Creamed Spinach

Crepes Suzette Derby

Preheat the oven to 375° F. Wipe meat with a clean, dry cloth and season all over with salt and pepper. Heat the oil in a Dutch oven or heavy ovenproof covered pot over medium-high heat. Add the meat and brown it on all sides. Remove the meat to a platter.

Add onion, carrots, celery, and leek to the pot and sauté over medium heat, stirring, until the vegetables are lightly browned but not scorched, about 10 minutes. Add the flour and continue to sauté for about 2 more minutes. Add the wine, basil, bay leaf, tomatoes, tomato purée, garlic, paprika, celery salt, and stock. Return the meat to the pot and bring to a gentle boil. Carefully skim off foam and excess fat. Cover the pot tightly, place in oven, and cook for 2 hours and 40 minutes or until meat is tender.

Remove the meat to a platter and strain sauce through a sieve, pushing down on the vegetables to extract all their juice; discard vegetables. Slice the meat and spoon some of the sauce over meat; pass additional sauce at the table. Serve with Brown Derby Potato Pancakes (recipe follows).

Potato Pancakes

2 EGGS, WELL BEATEN

$1/4$ TEASPOON NUTMEG

1 TEASPOON FINELY CHOPPED PARSLEY

3 POTATOES, PEELED AND FINELY GRATED

2 TABLESPOONS ALL-PURPOSE FLOUR

$1/2$ TEASPOON BAKING POWDER

SALT

$1/2$ CUP BUTTER, CLARIFIED

Preheat the oven to low. Beat together eggs, nutmeg, parsley, and potatoes. Add flour, baking powder, and salt to taste; blend until smooth. Melt the butter in a heavy skillet over medium-high heat. When butter begins to bubble, drop in a tablespoonful for each cake, pressing gently with back of spoon to spread evenly. Sauté until golden brown, about 3 minutes, then turn and cook on second side. Keep the pancakes warm in the oven until all are made.

Charlie Chaplin and Paulette Goddard
The great film genius and his wife were always the center of attention when they appeared in Hollywood. Paulette starred with the "Little Tramp" in Chaplin's brilliant satire on mass production, *Modern Times*, in 1936. It was also the film that began Chaplin's reputation as a nonconformist. His individuality is apparent even here, where he is without the necktie that was otherwise always required under the Brown Derby's dress code.

Charles Chaplin

Robert Taylor and Barbara Stanwyck

Taylor and Stanwyck were one of the most photographed couples in Hollywood, and it was often at the Brown Derby that the photographers found them. They were in love onscreen in *This Is My Affair* in 1937 and were married two years later. Taylor joined the Navy in 1943, and presented Stanwyck with a diamond-and-ruby-studded locket before their farewell dinner at the Hollywood Brown Derby. They were two of Hollywood's most enduring stars. Barbara Stanwyck was one of the screen's great leading ladies, while Robert Taylor, with his perfect features, was one of MGM's favorite leading men for twenty-five years.

Filet Mignon Tidbits

SERVES 4

Barbara Stanwyck and Robert Taylor liked to share a late-night supper of Filet Mignon Tidbits, one of the Brown Derby's Specialties of the House.

1 POUND THINLY SLICED FILET OF BEEF
MARINADE
1/2 CUP OLIVE OIL
1/2 CUP WINE VINEGAR
1 CUP WATER
1 TABLESPOON BLACK PEPPERCORNS
1 MEDIUM ONION, SLICED
2 CLOVES GARLIC
1/2 GREEN BELL PEPPER, SLICED
1 CUP BURGUNDY WINE

2 1/2 TABLESPOONS SALT
3 TABLESPOONS BARBEQUE SPICES, COMMERICAL OR
SEE BELOW
FINISHING THE DISH
4 TABLESPOONS BUTTER
1 TEASPOON WORCESTERSHIRE SAUCE
6 LARGE MUSHROOMS, SLICED
1/2 CUP BROWN GRAVY
1 TEASPOON BROWN MUSTARD
2 TABLESPOONS A-1 SAUCE

Cut the beef into thin strips, pat them dry, and place in a glass, porcelain, or stainless steel bowl or pan. Combine the marinade ingredients well and pour over beef. Cover with plastic wrap and store in the refrigerator overnight or for 8 to 10 hours.

Remove the tidbits from the marinade and dry them well on paper towels. Heat the butter in a heavy skillet over medium-high heat. Add the meat and mushrooms, and sauté quickly, about 3 to 4 minutes, until just cooked. Whisk together the wine, mustard, Worcestershire, Brown Gravy, and A-1 Sauce, and add the mixture to the tidbits. Bring just to a simmer, then remove to a heated serving dish or chafing dish and serve at once over steamed rice or rice cooked in chicken broth.

Barbeque Spices

2 TABLESPOONS CHILE POWDER
1 TEASPOON CELERY SALT
1 TEASPOON GARLIC SALT
1 TEASPOON GROUND CORIANDER
2 TEASPOONS PAPRIKA
1 TEASPOON SALT
1 TEASPOON PEPPER

Mix all the ingredients together. Reserve the excess for future use.

John Wayne

John Wayne and Josephine Saenz Wayne

Wayne and Josephine, his first wife, entered the Hollywood Derby for dinner after having cocktails in the Bamboo Room. Handsome and rugged, the "Duke" had his first big success in John Ford's *Stagecoach* in 1939. He became an American icon with his performances as the heroic figure in films such as *Flying Tigers*, *Rio Bravo*, and *The Searchers*. Josie and John Wayne had four children during an eleven-year marriage that ended in 1944. Wayne married twice more. He and Pilar, his last wife, with whom he had three more children, lived in Newport Beach. Still larger than life after forty years in the movies, he won the Oscar for *True Grit* in 1969. Wayne died in 1979 at the age of 72.

𝒟esi Arnaz and Lucille Ball Lucy was a starlet when she first came into the Brown Derby in the thirties. In those days, she and Betty Grable would come in together hoping to be discovered by a producer. By the 1940s she was a star at MGM and married to Desi.

On January 19, 1953, Desi Arnaz rushed into the Hollywood Brown Derby, threw his arms into the air and shouted, "Now we got everythin'!" Lucy had given birth that morning to their son, Desi, Jr. That same night, on one of the highest-rated shows in television history, the couple's alter egos, the Ricardos, had a son on "I Love Lucy."

*J*ane Wyman and Ronald Reagan
Wyman and Reagan enjoyed a game of gin,
which was popular in the 1940s, after dinner
at the Hollywood Derby. Ronnie and Janie, as I
knew them, were both contract players at
Warner Brothers when they were married in
1940. The following year Ronnie gave perhaps
his finest film performance in *King's Row*.
Janie's talent as a great dramatic actress was
revealed in Billy Wilder's *The Lost Weekend* in
1945. She received her first nomination as
Best Actress for *The Yearling* and won the
Oscar two years later for her stunning portrayal of a deaf mute in *Johnny Belinda*.
The Reagans were one of Hollywood's favorite
young couples and the film community was
sorry to hear the news when they divorced in
1948.

Ronald Reagan   Jane Wyman

Catalina Sand Dabs

SERVES 4

Ron Reagan and Jane Wyman loved the Brown Derby Catalina Sand Dabs Meuniere. The sand dabs were always the freshest possible, served just hours after being caught off the coast of Catalina Island. If you are fortunate enough to obtain the fish, they are superb when prepared simply as they were at the Derby.

3 POUNDS SAND DAB FILLETS
$1/_2$ CUP MILK
$1/_2$ CUP ALL-PURPOSE FLOUR
SALT
$1/_2$ CUP BUTTER, CLARIFIED
1 TEASPOON FINELY CHOPPED PARSLEY
JUICE OF 1 LEMON

Wash the sand dabs carefully in cold water, then pat them dry. Dip fillets in milk, roll in flour, and salt lightly. Melt the butter in a heavy skillet over medium-high heat. When butter just begins to bubble, add the fish and sauté until golden brown on each side; do not overcook. Sprinkle with parsley and lemon juice, pour the butter remaining in the skillet over the fish and serve immediately.

This recipe becomes Sand Dabs Almandine by sprinkling the sautéed fish with toasted sliced almonds.

Old-Fashioned Navy Bean Soup

SERVES 8

1 CUP DRIED NAVY BEANS
$1/4$ CUP JULIENNED LEEKS, WHITE PORTIONS ONLY
$1/4$ CUP BUTTER
2 QUARTS CHICKEN OR BEEF STOCK
$1/2$ CUP DICED CARROTS
1 SMOKED HAM HOCK
$1/2$ CUP DICED CELERY
2 MEDIUM TOMATOES, PEELED, SEEDED, AND DICED
$1/2$ CUP DICED ONION
1 TABLESPOON CHOPPED PARSLEY

Soak beans in cold water for 8 hours. Heat butter in a large kettle over medium heat. Add carrots, celery, onion, and leeks; cover and braise 5 minutes without browning.

Drain beans and rinse thoroughly. Add beans, stock, and ham hock to kettle and cook 1 $1/2$ hours, stirring occasionally, until the beans are tender. Add tomatoes and parsley; simmer another 30 minutes. Remove the ham hock. Trim the meat from the bone, dice it finely and return it to the soup; discard bone.

Walt and Lillian Disney

The genius of Walt Disney was already known and loved around the world when he and his wife, Lillian, were photographed at the Hollywood Brown Derby in 1939. A year earlier, Walt Disney Studios had released the first animated feature film, *Snow White*, an enormous artistic and commercial success. Walt's best-known character, Mickey Mouse, was created two years after his marriage to Lillian in 1925, and it was Lillian who was responsible for Disney changing the name of the new character from Mortimer Mouse to Mickey Mouse.

Walt and Bob Cobb were friends who also shared a love of baseball. They served together on the board of directors of the Pacific Coast League's Hollywood Stars and on the advisory board of Gene Autry's California Angels. In 1955, Bob and I were invited to the opening of Disneyland, which was the realization of Walt's dream. We stopped in to congratulate him at his private office above the old firehouse and were thrilled to look out over Main Street at the spectacular celebration in Walt's Magic Kingdom.

Betty Grable

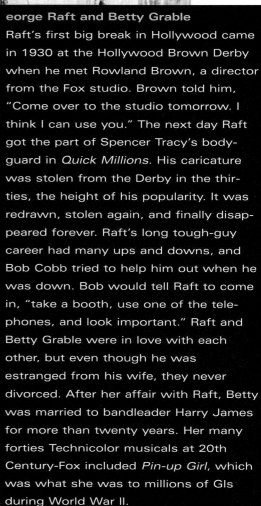

George Raft and Betty Grable

Raft's first big break in Hollywood came in 1930 at the Hollywood Brown Derby when he met Rowland Brown, a director from the Fox studio. Brown told him, "Come over to the studio tomorrow. I think I can use you." The next day Raft got the part of Spencer Tracy's bodyguard in *Quick Millions*. His caricature was stolen from the Derby in the thirties, the height of his popularity. It was redrawn, stolen again, and finally disappeared forever. Raft's long tough-guy career had many ups and downs, and Bob Cobb tried to help him out when he was down. Bob would tell Raft to come in, "take a booth, use one of the telephones, and look important." Raft and Betty Grable were in love with each other, but even though he was estranged from his wife, they never divorced. After her affair with Raft, Betty was married to bandleader Harry James for more than twenty years. Her many forties Technicolor musicals at 20th Century-Fox included *Pin-up Girl*, which was what she was to millions of GIs during World War II.

Bing and Dixie Crosby leaving the Hollywood Brown Derby Bing and Dixie always entertained beautifully at their house in Holmby Hills. I'll always remember the last birthday party that Dixie gave for Bing. Their old friends were there, in the house that had held so many marvelous parties. Dixie, who loved orchids, surrounded us all with the most extravagant display of phaleonopsis and cymbidiums that I've ever seen. In time, the old house was taken down and Aaron Spelling built one of the largest residences in Los Angeles on the site.

Roast Duck Derby

SERVES 4 TO 6

Bob Cobb and Bing Crosby hunted together often. After one of their more successful shoots, Bing celebrated at the Hollywood Brown Derby with a roast duck dinner for his friends. The kitchen cleaned the birds and the chef prepared them so perfectly that Bing never forgot it.

1 (5-6 POUND) DUCK, DRAWN
1 SPRIG THYME
SALT AND PEPPER
1 CUP PORT
4 CUPS BROWN DERBY DRESSING (PAGE 48)
JUICE AND PEEL OF 1 ORANGE
$^1/_4$ CUP WATER
2 CUPS BROWN GRAVY
1 MEDIUM ONION, CUT IN $^1/_2$-INCH PIECES
1 CUP CHICKEN BROTH OR WATER
2 STALKS CELERY, CUT IN $^1/_2$-INCH PIECES
2 TABLESPOONS RED CURRANT JELLY
2 MEDIUM CARROTS, CUT IN $^1/_2$-INCH PIECES
$^1/_4$ TEASPOON GROUND GINGER
1 BAY LEAF
4 TABLESPOONS BUTTER
12 PEPPERCORNS

Preheat oven to 400°F. Wash and dry the duck well and season it inside and out with salt and pepper. Stuff the duck with Brown Derby Dressing and tie securely. Place in roasting pan and baste with $^1/_4$ cup water. Roast in the oven until golden brown (approximately 15 minutes). Reduce heat to 350°F and add onion, celery, carrots, bay leaf, peppercorns, and thyme to the roasting pan. Cover and roast for 1 hour and 40 minutes, basting frequently.

Remove excess fat from the pan drippings and add the wine, orange juice, Brown Sauce, chicken broth, currant jelly, and ground ginger; continue to roast, covered, for 20 minutes longer, basting frequently.

Meanwhile, remove the zest from the orange, preferably with a potato peeler, avoiding the white pith. Cut the zest into $^1/_8$-inch-wide julienne strips. Place

strips in a small pot with enough water to cover and bring to a boil. Drain and refresh zest under cold water.

When the duck is done, transfer it to a heated platter and remove the string. Strain the drippings through a fine sieve, remove excess fat again, and bring to a boil. To finish the sauce, add the butter bit by bit, whisking vigorously until completely incorporated. Add the julienned zest to the sauce and taste for seasonings. Glaze the duck with a little gravy and serve the remainder at the table.

*P*hil Harris, Bing Crosby, et al. It was the "morning after" a duck dinner in the American Room of the Hollywood Brown Derby and it looks as though they had a wonderful time the night before. Phil Harris often hunted with Bob and Bing. He and his wife, Alice Faye, lived in Palm Springs and often spent the night in town after social or business engagements. When they did, they invariably stopped at the Derby for brunch before heading back to the desert.

Edward G. Robinson

&dward G. and Gladys Robinson
The Robinsons attended an after-the
ater supper party at the Hollywood
Brown Derby. Robinson is most ofte
remembered for his portrayals of
tough guys, but in fact he was one
the most cultured actors in Hollywo
The first of his gangster roles was ir
Mervyn LeRoy's *Little Caesar*, one o
the best crime films of all time. An
actor of great versatility, he later
appeared in *Double Indemnity* and
Cecil B. DeMille's *The Ten
Commandments*.

Robinson's French Impressior
paintings were part of one of the mo
outstanding private art collections in
the United States. They were sold in
the Robinsons' divorce settlement in
1957.

Veal Paprika

SERVES 4

Edward G. Robinson was born Manny Goldenberg in Bucharest, Romania, in 1893. The Brown Derby's Veal Paprika was based on his family recipe for his favorite dish.

1 1/2 POUNDS THIN VEAL CUTLETS
1/4 CUP CLARIFIED BUTTER
1 TABLESPOON SWEET HUNGARIAN PAPRIKA
1 TEASPOON FINELY CHOPPED ONION
1 CUP HEAVY CREAM
1/2 CUP BROWN GRAVY
SALT AND PEPPER

Flatten the cutlets until they are very thin. Heat butter in a large heavy skillet over medium-high heat. Add cutlets and quickly sauté until golden brown on both sides, about 3 minutes total. Sprinkle with paprika, add onion, and cook, covered, 1 minute. Add the cream and Brown Gravy, and season with salt and pepper to taste. Bring just to a simmer. Remove the cutlets to a heated platter and keep warm. Simmer gravy until reduced by one third. Strain through a fine sieve. Spoon some of the sauce over the cutlets and pass the rest at the table. Serve with noodles or spaetzle.

AN ABOUT TOWN

Gregson—Greg—Bautzer was a prominent entertainment lawyer whose clients included Joseph Schenck and Howard Hughes; more recently, he represented Kirk Kerkorian in his takeover of MGM. Through the forties and fifties Bautzer also was a famously eligible bachelor. It was not unusual for him to have a business lunch at the Brown Derby only to return in the evening for a date with one of Hollywood's most beautiful women. Hedda Hopper and Louella Parsons routinely reported Bautzer's dates and romances, especially those with glamorous movie stars.

One of those was Lana Turner, (above) who met the handsome young attorney in 1938, when she was seventeen years old and playing bit parts for Mervyn LeRoy at MGM—she said Bautzer was her first love. The couple became engaged. Marriage, however, seemed less appealing to Bautzer than engagements, and Turner finally broke it off to marry band leader Artie Shaw, the first of her seven husbands. Turner became one of MGM's biggest stars. Some of her great roles were in *The Postman Always Rings Twice* opposite John Garfield and in Vincente Minelli's *The Bad and the Beautiful.*

Greg was so in love with Dorothy Lamour (below) and she with him that when they became engaged, everyone in Hollywood thought they would marry. Dorothy and Greg were together at the Derby constantly. The war interfered with their romance, though. Dorothy's popularity was at its height then and her cross-country tours

set a record for war bond sales. She met a handsome captain named Bill Howard, and they were married in 1943. Dorothy and Bill had two sons and a long and happy marriage that lasted until Bill's death.

Joan Crawford, (above) shown here wearing her famous star sapphire, had an intense and much publicized affair with Greg in the mid-forties; her Oscar-winning performance in *Mildred Pierce* (1945) had put her back on top in Hollywood and back in the media spotlight. The couple was often photographed at nightclubs and film premiers. Several years later though, Crawford married Alfred Steele, the president of Pepsi-Cola.

Ginger Rogers (below) and Greg dated for a time after Ginger's divorce from Jack Briggs in 1948. In addition to Greg's romantic interest, Greg also represented Ginger legally as he had done with Lana Turner and Joan Crawford. In 1949 Ginger Rogers was reunited with Fred Astaire after ten years for their final film together, *The Barkleys of Broadway*. Greg was finally married for the first time in the 1950s to the actress Dana Wynter, with whom he had a son. At the time of his death in 1988 he was married to Niki Dantine, daughter of Nicholas M. Schenck, the former president of Loew's Inc.

The Beverly Hills Brown Derby

*A*S BEVERLY HILLS became the place for the movie colony to live, it became important to have a local Brown Derby. The city of Beverly Hills was still developing in 1931 when Bob Cobb opened the Beverly Hills Brown Derby on the corner of Wilshire Boulevard and Rodeo Drive, directly across the street from the Beverly Wilshire Hotel. The restaurant became increasingly popular as Rodeo Drive became the Fifth Avenue of Los Angeles, but it retained more of a neighborhood feeling than the Vine Street location. Thursday evening was always busy and it was also the best night to see the stars since that was the maid's night out. The Brown Derby was a landmark in Beverly Hills and a favorite with area residents for more than fifty years until it closed in 1982.

𝒯he Academy Room in the Beverly Hills Brown Derby
All the Best Actor and Best Actress Academy Award winners were honored with charcoal portraits by the artist Volpe which lined the walls.

R obert Wagner and Natalie Wood
Natalie Wood was nineteen when
she and Robert Wagner were married
on December 28, 1957. Louella
Parsons reported to the nation that
"the happy bride-and-groom-to-be
had dinner at the Brown Derby, then
took off by train Thursday night for
Scottsdale, Arizona, for the big wedding Saturday." They wanted to be
married out of town to avoid having
the event turned into a spectacle.
The original plan was to drive, but
sixteen pieces of luggage made that
impractical. The train was the answer
and R. J. arranged for compartments,
complete with fresh flowers, on the
Southern Pacific "Golden State."

Joanne Woodward and James W. Warren
In 1957 Joanne Woodward won an
Academy Award for her portrayal of a schiz-
ophrenic in *The Three Faces of Eve*; she and
James W. Warren, Vice President of the
Brown Derbies, were present when her portrait was placed in the Academy Room. The
following year she and Paul Newman were
married and the couple starred in the first of
their many films together, *The Long Hot
Summer*.

R*andolph Scott, Phyllis and Fred Astaire, Liz Whitney*
Fred Astaire was a Beverly Hills resident for fifty years. When he dined at one of the Derbies, it was usually the one in Beverly Hills and often with very good friends. Here he is with his first wife, Phyllis, and Liz Whitney (the former Mrs. Jock Whitney) and Randolph Scott in 1941. Fred and Randy Scott, who both loved simple meals like steak and vegetables, were also on screen together in *Follow the Fleet*, one of the unforgettable Fred Astaire and Ginger Rogers musicals of the thirties.
In 1962, Randy was having lunch in the Beverly Derby with the director Sam Peckinpah and Joel McCrea. Randy and Joel were costarring in Peckinpah's western *Ride the High Country*. Because of a hearing problem, Randy thought he and Joel were flipping a coin for the check, but it was actually for top billing. Randy won the toss, and the film, which won First Prize at the Cannes Film Festival, is considered the finest of his career.

Greer Garson and Gary Cooper

Gary Cooper, the personification of the All-American male, and Greer Garson were two of Hollywood's most popular stars and were also among the most highly honored members of the Academy of Motion Pictures Art and Sciences. Cooper won Best Actor Oscars for *Sergeant York* (1941) and *High Noon* (1952), and an Honorary Award in 1960. Garson, nominated for Best Actress six times, including for *Goodbye Mr. Chips*, won for her role in *Mrs. Miniver*, the most popular film of 1942. Cooper and Bob Cobb, both born in Montana and both cowboys early in life, were longtime friends.

atalie Draper, Patricia Stillman and Mrs. William Hawks (opposite). Gloria Vanderbilt, Sally Wright Cobb, Jayne Larkin Wrightsman (above)

I was a frequent visitor to the Brown Derby before I ever met Bob Cobb. I would meet my girlfriends for lunch at the Beverly Hills Brown Derby two or three times a week. Our crowd included the actress Natalie Draper, Patricia Stillman, Gloria Vanderbilt, and Jayne Larkin. Later on Natalie Draper married writer and producer Ivan Goff and then attorney Henry M. Moffat. Patricia Stillman was Mrs. Randolph Scott from 1944 until Randy's death. Gloria Vanderbilt's first husband was Pat de Cicco. Jayne Larkin married the New York financier Charles Wrightsman. Jayne assembled one of the world's foremost collections of eighteenth-century French furniture and decorative arts — the Wrightsman Collection is now on permanent display at New York's Metropolitan Museum of Art. I was the last to marry when I married Bob Cobb in 1945.

Maureen O'Sullivan and John Farrow

The actress Maureen O'Sullivan and her husband John Farrow posed for the Derby's photographer as they were leaving the Beverly Hills Derby—a uniformed page had just let them know that their car had arrived. O'Sullivan was Jane to Johnny Weissmuller's *Tarzan* in MGM's hugely popular Tarzan jungle adventures. She married Farrow, an established screenwriter, in 1936. The following year he began a successful career as a director that included films such as *Wake Island* and *Hondo*. Their daughter, Mia, had her screen debut in Farrow's last film, *John Paul Jones*, in 1959— she was thirteen years old. In 1986, O'Sullivan played Mia's mother in Woody Allen's *Hannah and Her Sisters*.

Judy Garland
On a break during the filming of *The Wizard of Oz*, Judy Garland stepped out of the Brown Derby onto Rodeo Drive through our famous revolving door, the first in the city of Beverly Hills. Judy's next film was *Babes in Arms* with Mickey Rooney, the beginning of a series of MGM musicals that teamed the juvenile stars. Judy, Mickey, and their young friends made up a regular Sunday morning breakfast crowd that met at the Beverly Derby. *Babes in Arms* opened in 1939 at Grauman's Chinese Theater on Hollywood Boulevard, just a few blocks away from the Hollywood Brown Derby. After the premier, Judy's footprints were immortalized in the concrete outside the theater.

The Derby House

The Derby House, furnished in Olde English style, opened in 1938 as an extension to the Beverly Hills Derby. Though open to the public, the intimate room was often used for private parties.

Paulette Goddard, Sylvia Ashley, Douglas Fairbanks, Merle Oberon, Alexander Korda

This supper party given by director Alexander Korda and his wife, Merle Oberon, was held at the Derby House of the Beverly Hills Brown Derby in 1939. This was one of the last photographs taken of Douglas Fairbanks, Sr., before his sudden heart attack and death at age fifty-five. Five years earlier, in his final film role, the dashing hero of the silent screen had costarred with the beautiful Oberon in Korda's film *The Private Life of Don Juan*. Sylvia Ashley, three of whose five husbands were titled, went on to marry Clark Gable in 1949.

Douglas Fairbanks

Reginald Gardiner, Richard Greene, Charles Ruggles

The bar at the Derby House was a popular spot with the Hollywood set, including actors Reginald Gardiner, Richard Greene, and Charles Ruggles. The Brown Derby stocked its own private-label wines and liquors in addition to an extensive wine list

Brown Derby
PUERTO RICAN RUM
WHITE LABEL

DISTILLED AND BOTTLED SPECIALLY FOR
The Brown Derby
HOLLYWOOD
CALIFORNIA

BY BRUGAL & CO., C. POR A, RIO PIEDRAS, PUERTO RICO, NO. 2, LTD.
© 1940 BY THE BROWN DERBY CORPORATION

4/5 QUART

STORAGE TANK Nº 25
CAP 1024 GAL.

11.8.40

BROWN DERBY

(RESERVE)

Brown Derby wines were bottled by the Beaulieu Vineyard winery in Rutherford, Napa Valley, California. Here, Bob Cobb is shown on a visit to the vineyard and its cellars in 1940.

Spaghetti Derby

SERVES 8 TO 10

The pasta served at the Derby was spaghetti, and it was served with style—not tossed together, but layered. First the spaghetti was prepared al dente and tossed in butter, then topped with Brown Derby Tomato Sauce, and finished with Brown Derby Meat Sauce. Grated aged Parmesan cheese was sprinkled on top. Rosalind Russell preferred her spaghetti simply tossed in butter, but it was the sauces that made our Spaghetti Derby famous. Spaghetti Derby was also Joan Bennett's favorite; she liked to begin the meal with a crisp green salad.

Brown Derby Meat Sauce

MAKES 1 QUART

1 POUND GROUND BEEF	1 (16-OUNCE) CAN WHOLE TOMATOES
1 POUND GROUND VEAL	2 CUPS BEEF STOCK
1/2 POUND GROUND PORK	1/2 TEASPOON OREGANO
1/2 CUP OLIVE OIL	1/2 TEASPOON BASIL
1 LARGE ONION, CHOPPED	1/4 TEASPOON NUTMEG
2 CLOVES GARLIC, CHOPPED	1 BAY LEAF
1/2 POUND FRESH MUSHROOMS SLICED	1/4 TEASPOON ROSEMARY
1 OUNCE CHOPPED DRY MUSHROOMS	1/2 TABLESPOON SWEET PAPRIKA
1 CUP BURGUNDY	1 TEASPOON SALT
1 (16 OUNCE) CAN TOMATO PURÉE	1 TABLESPOON GROUND BLACK PEPPER

Preheat the oven to 350° F. Pat the meat into a roasting pan or large skillet and place it in the oven. Brown the meat, stirring often to get an even color. Heat oil in a heavy kettle. Add onion, garlic, and mushrooms; sauté 5 minutes, stirring well. Add wine, purée, toma-toes, and beef stock; simmer 10 minutes. Add browned meat and spices; simmer gently over low heat 1 1/2 hours.

Brown Derby Tomato Sauce

MAKES 1 ¹/₂ QUARTS

¹/₂ CUP OLIVE OIL
¹/₂ LARGE ONION, CHOPPED
1 CLOVE GARLIC, CHOPPED
1 SMALL CARROT, DICED
2 OUTER STALKS CELERY, DICED
¹/₂ TABLESPOON BLACK PEPPERCORNS
1 HAM HOCK

1 (28-OUNCE) CAN TOMATO PURÉE
1 (28-OUNCE) CAN WHOLE TOMATOES
¹/₄ TEASPOON THYME
¹/₄ TEASPOON BASIL
¹/₄ TEASPOON OREGANO
1 TEASPOON SALT
¹/₂ CUP ALL-PURPOSE FLOUR

Heat olive oil in a heavy kettle over medium heat. Add onion, garlic, carrot, celery, peppercorns, and ham hock; sauté 8 minutes. Add the flour and blend well. Add purée, tomatoes, spices, and salt; simmer gently 1 hour. Strain through a fine sieve. This sauce is also great for meat, fish, or poultry.

Beverly Salad Bowl

SERVES 4

1 MEDIUM HEAD ROMAINE
¹/₄ HEAD ICEBERG LETTUCE
¹/₄ BUNCH WATERCRESS
¹/₂ BUNCH FLAT-LEAF PARSLEY
2 CUPS SHREDDED CABBAGE

4 OUNCES LEAN BAKED HAM, JULIENNED
4 OUNCES SWISS CHEESE, JULIENNED
4 OUNCES WHITE MEAT OF CHICKEN, JULIENNED
2 HARD COOKED EGGS, SLICED
2 TABLESPOONS CHOPPED CHIVES

³/₄ CUP COBB'S OLD-FASHIONED FRENCH DRESSING (PAGE 18)

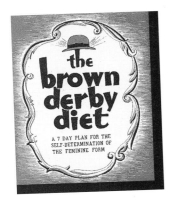

Cut romaine, iceberg lettuce, watercress, and parsley into 1-inch pieces and toss together in a chilled salad bowl with the cabbage and French Dressing. Top with ham, cheese, and chicken, arranged in wedges. Garnish with the sliced eggs, and sprinkle with chopped chives.

Rosalind Russell and Fred Brisson
Rosalind Russell lived in Beverly Hills and she and Freddie Brisson were regulars at the Beverly Hills Derby even before they were married. Cary Grant introduced the couple when he and Rosalind were filming *His Girl Friday* for Howard Hawks in 1939. Rosalind and Freddie were newlyweds when this picture was taken in 1941; their marriage lasted more than thirty years.

Olivia De Havilland and Jimmy Stewart
A few weeks after he and Olivia De
Havilland stopped into the Beverly Hills
Brown Derby for dinner, Jimmy Stewart
won the 1940 Academy Award for his performance in *The Philadelphia Story*. Olivia
had been nominated the year before for her
supporting role as Melanie in David O.
Selznick's *Gone with the Wind*. Before the
end of the decade, she won two Best
Actress Oscars for *To Each His Own* (1946)
and *The Heiress* (1949).

    Jimmy's classic films, including
Mr. Smith Goes to Washington and Frank
Capra's *It's a Wonderful Life*, have made
him one of America's best loved actors. He
and his wife, Gloria, whom he married in
1949, were one of Hollywood's best loved
couples

Olivia de Havilland   James Stewart

Hollywood Style

During Hollywood's Golden Age, movie stars in public were as glamourous as they were on the screen - they seemed to think they owed as much to their fans. They set an example for the rest of us. Above, from left: Tony Martin and his first wife, Alice Fay; Bob and Sally Cobb; Fay Wray and Delores Del Rio. Opposite, from left: Ruth Warrick; Sheila Graham and Zsz Zsa Gabor; Gary Cooper and Mary Pickford; George Hamilton and Susan Kohner.

Dorothy Lamour and Edith Head

Edith Head was nominated thirty-three times for costume design and won eight Academy Awards during her extraordinary career. She and the exotic Dorothy Lamour first met in 1936, when Edith designed her famous sarong for Paramount's *Jungle Princess*. It was Edith's inspiration to adapt the traditional cotton sarong to the one made of satin crepe that draped beautifully over Dorothy's body. The film made Dorothy a star, and the sarong became her trademark in a number of films, including John Ford's *The Hurricane* in 1937.

The 1959 Academy Awards ceremony was held at the Pantages Theater on Hollywood Boulevard. Preceding the Oscar telecast, which Edith called "the greatest fashion show in the world," NBC broadcast a half-hour pre-Oscar party from the Hollywood Brown Derby. Betsy Palmer and Tony Randall were co-hosts and all the major nominees were invited to attend. Edith Head, the official design consultant for the Academy of Motion Picture Arts and Sciences, was on hand to describe to the television audience what the nominees were wearing.

Oleg Cassini and Gene Tierney

Gene Tierney was just twenty years old and beginning her rise to stardom when she met Oleg Cassini, who was twenty-eight, the son of a Russian countess, and a costume designer at Paramount; the year was 1940. During their marriage, which lasted from 1941 to 1952, Cassini designed costumes for Tierney in such films as *Shanghai Gesture* and *The Razor's Edge*. She was unforgettable in Otto Preminger's classic, haunting mystery, *Laura* (1944), and in her most popular film *Leave Her to Heaven* (1945). Cassini hit the height of his fame in fashion as Jacqueline Kennedy's principal designer during her years as First Lady.

$\mathscr{D}$orothy Lamour and Rita Hayworth

THe glamourous stars paused for a moment to be photographed in the Los Feliz Brown Derby in 1942. Gorgeous Rita Hayworth, also a gifted dancer, played opposite Fred Astaire later that year in *You Were Never Lovelier*. America's love goddess in the 1940s, Rita was immortalized as *Gilda*, with Glenn Ford, in 1947.

Dorothy's gift for light comedy was perfect for the series of Road pictures she made with Bob Hope and Bing Crosby. First teamed in the *Road to Singapore* in 1940, they continued together on the roads to Morocco, Zanzibar, Singapore, Utopia, Rio, and Bali.

Shrimp Creole with Rice

SERVES 4

Dorothy Lamour, who was Miss New Orleans in 1931, contributed this recipe for New Orleans Shrimp Creole to the Brown Derby's menu.

1 POUND LARGE SHRIMP, SHELLED AND DEVEINED
4 TABLESPOONS BUTTER, CLARIFIED
$^1/_2$ CUP WHITE WINE
2 CUPS CREOLE SAUCE (RECIPE FOLLOWS)

Bring a pot of water to a boil, add shrimp, and boil for 1 minute; drain shrimp, refresh them under cold water, and pat dry. Heat butter in heavy skillet over medium-high heat. Add shrimp and brown lightly, 30 to 40 seconds. Add wine, raise heat to high, and reduce by two-thirds. Add the sauce and cook for 5 minutes over medium heat. Serve with steamed rice.

Spanish or Creole Sauce

MAKES 2 CUPS

1 $^1/_2$ TABLESPOONS OLIVE OIL
1 CUP HAM TRIMMINGS OR SALT PORK, CHOPPED
1 CUP THINLY SLICED ONION
4 CLOVES GARLIC, FINELY CHOPPED
1 CUP JULIENNED CELERY
1 CUP JULIENNED GREEN PEPPER
$^1/_2$ CUP ALL-PURPOSE FLOUR
$^1/_2$ TEASPOON THYME
$^1/_2$ TEASPOON OREGANO

1 TEASPOON FILÉ
1 CUP WHITE WINE
2 CUPS CHICKEN STOCK
1 TABLESPOONS CELERY SALT
2 CUPS TOMATOES, FRESH OR SOLID PACK
1 CUP TOMATO PURÉE
$^1/_8$ TEASPOON TABASCO OR SIMILAR HOT PEPPER SAUCE
2 TABLESPOONS SALT
1 BAY LEAF

Heat olive oil in heavy kettle over medium heat. Add ham trimmings and sauté until lightly browned. Add onion and garlic and continue cooking until lightly browned. Add celery and green pepper, mixing well, and sauté 5 minutes more. Add flour, thyme, oregano, and filé and cook over medium-low heat for 3 minutes. Add wine, stock, celery salt, tomatoes, tomato purée, Tabasco, salt, and bay leaf. Cook 30 minutes over low heat.

*L*oretta Young, Ann Southern, Mal Milland, Lillian MacMurray

In 1940 women wore hats. It was a happy time for these Hollywood wives when Ann Southern (Mrs. Roger Pryor) gave a baby shower for Ray Milland's wife, Mal, in the American Room. Loretta Young and Lillian MacMurray—who was married to Fred MacMurray—joined in the ceremony of cutting the Brown Derby's famous Candy Ribbon Cake.

GENTLEMEN!

In deference to the ladies, the Management respectfully requests Gentlemen patrons of the Cocktail Lounge to remove their hats.

The BROWN DERBY

*H*at or no hat, who could possibly choose a favorite from these handsome leading men? From left: Clark Gable, Fred MacMurray, and Cary Grant.

SUNDAY

DEAR SIR:—

I HAVE JUST COME BACK FROM THE PACIFIC AND MY BUDDY WHO DIED OUT THERE ASKED ME IF I EVER GOT TO HOLLYWOOD TO DO HIM A FAVOR AND PAY BACK A DEBT. HE GAVE ME TWO DOLLARS AND ASKED ME TO GIVE IT TO THE BOSS AT THE BROWN DERBY IN HOLLYWOOD

SEEMS MY PAL WAS HUNGRY A FEW YEARS AGO AND WENT TO YOUR PLACE AND ATE A LOT OF FOOD AND COULDN'T PAY FOR IT AND YOU LET HIM GET BY WITH IT AND DIDN'T

CALL THE POLICE AND HE ASKED ME TO LOOK YOU UP IF I EVER GOT TO HOLLYWOOD AND HE ASKED ME TO EXPLAIN AND SAY HE WAS SORRY — THEN HE DIED.

I TELEPHONED YOU TODAY AND GOT YOUR NAME FROM THE GIRL ON THE PHONE — BUT SHE SAID YOU WOULD NOT BE AROUND TODAY.

I WANTED TO EXPLAIN EVERYTHING TO YOU BUT I GUESS THIS NOTE WILL HAVE TO DO THE EXPLAINING FOR MY BUDDY AS I AM SHOVING OFF TOMORROW.

IF I EVER GET BACK THIS WAY I HOPE I CAN MEET YOU.

YOURS TRULY

JOE RYAN

One night two young servicemen had dinner at the Hollywood Brown Derby and asked to speak to Bob. The young men explained that they had wanted their last dinner in the States to be in the famous Brown Derby they had always read about. They had dined on steaks and champagne and finished with cigars, but they couldn't pay their bill. They were shipping out the next morning, and needless to say Bob was touched. They sat and talked until the soldiers needed

The War Years

Three days after the attack on Pearl Harbor on December 7, 1941, the Hollywood Victory Committee was established to support the war effort and entertain the armed forces. Hollywood played host to the huge number of servicemen stationed in and shipped out of Southern California. In the Hollywood Brown Derby, uniforms were a familiar sight. Of course, some of the men in uniform had been celebrities in private life, and the stars who joined the service included Jimmy Stewart, William Holden, Tyrone Power, and Henry Fonda. Clark Gable enlisted in the Air Force after Carole Lombard, Hollywood's first war casualty, was killed in a plane crash on her return home from a campaign to sell war bonds. The Brown Derby maintained the highest standards possible under wartime rationing and food scarcities, and waitresses began to outnumber waiters at the Hollywood Derby as more and more men were called up.

Many of the Armed Forces Radio Service shows that were broadcast around the world originated from the CBS Radio Playhouse Theater, directly across Vine Street from the Hollywood Brown Derby. In hundreds of broadcasts throughout the war, there were performances by almost every major star in show business. And the stars would usually stop into the Brown Derby before or after their show. When victory in Europe was declared, the Official Army-Navy Program for VE-Day was broadcast from the CBS Radio Playhouse, with Meredith Willson conducting. The Brown Derby was a virtual canteen for the one hundred stars who participated in that historic event. Vine Street was blocked off between Sunset and Hollywood and there was dancing in the street in the emotional celebration that ensued.

WESTERN UNION

SYMBOLS
DL=Day Letter
NL=Overnight Telegram
LC=Deferred Cable
NLT=Cable Night Letter

SZ349 70 DL=WUX HOLLYWOOD CALIF 19 416P   1943 JUL 19 PM 7 04
MR BOB COBB=
    BROWN DERBY RESTAURANT 1628 NORTH VINE ST   HD=

THERE WAS AN OLD LADY WHO LIVED IN A SHOE SHE HAD SO MANY
MOUTHS TO FEED SHE DIDN'T KNOW WHAT TO DO. AND IF REPORTS ARE
CORRECT SHE HAD NOTHING ON YOU. THEM MAY LIMIT YOUR MEAT
POINTS. BUT THEY CAN NEVER RATION THE GOOD WILL THAT HAS TURNED
A HAT INTO THE MOST FAMOUS RESTUARANT IN THE WORLD. HATS OFF
TO BE BROWN DERBY ON ITS TWENTIETH ANNIVERSARY=
    CECIL B DEMILLE.

$\mathscr{E}$dgar Bergen, Zsa Zsa Gabor and Eva Gabor
Young Hollywood stars joined in the war effort by selling bonds at the Hollywood Brown Derby. Eva Gabor (seated) was volunteering her time when she was visited by her sister Zsa Zsa and Edgar Bergen. Zsa Zsa was Miss Hungary of 1936 before coming to the United States just before the war. Famous for her many marriages, which began with Conrad Hilton, Zsa Zsa also was married for a time to George Sanders. Her younger sister, Eva, arrived in Hollywood in the late 1930s and was a Derby regular through the years.

Alan Ladd and Sue Carol
Ladd signed autographs for wartime fans before dinner at the Hollywood Brown Derby with his wife, actress-agent Sue Carol. After years of playing small parts, Ladd had become an overnight star under Sue's management in *This Gun for Hire* (1942), with Veronica Lake. In 1943, Ladd was drafted into the Army Air Force. Ten years later he gave his finest screen performance opposite Jean Arthur in George Stevens's classic western, *Shane*. Alan Ladd, Jr., Sue's stepson, was one of the most powerful men in Hollywood in the 1980s as President and CEO of MGM/UA.

*C*laudette Colbert and Captain George S. Welsh Colbert, one of Hollywood's biggest stars in the early 1940s, helped boost the morale of servicemen during the war with her personal appearances. Here she is pictured chatting with Captain George S. Welsh in 1942. She was also part of the film industry's war effort when she starred in David O. Selznick's *Since You Went Away*, a film that focused on the American home front. Colbert was most famous as one of Hollywood's greatest comediennes in films that included *It Happened One Night*, with Clark Gable, and Preston Sturges's 1942 classic The *Palm Beach Story*.

*R*onald Reagan and Jane Wyman
Four months after Pearl Harbor,
Reagan received his orders to report
for duty at Fort Mason. Ronald and
Jane had a farewell dinner at the
Brown Derby in Hollywood before dri-
ving to Glendale, where he boarded his
train. A few months later he was
transferred to Los Angeles and spent
the duration of the war in Air Force
Intelligence making training films and
documentaries. Jane went on a
national war bond tour and made
numerous USO appearances that
included singing to the soldiers at the
embarkation station as they departed
Los Angeles.

Families

Pat O'Brien with wife Eloise, Margaret Mavourneen, and Sean

Family man Pat O'Brien, his wife, Eloise, and their children, happily cooperated for this photograph after breakfast at the Beverly Hills Brown Derby in the late thirties. Pat and Eloise, the love of his life, went on to have two more children and raised their family in a beautiful white colonial house in Brentwood.

Pat O'Brien, the son of Irish immigrants, was best known for his role as Notre Dame's famous football coach in *Knute Rockne–All American*. It was also the film in which twenty-nine-year-old Ronald Reagan, cast as George Gipp, delivered his famous line, "Win one for the Gipper."

Pat O'Brien

Corned Beef

SERVES 10 TO 12

Pat O'Brien loved the Brown Derby's corned beef.

1 (10- TO 12-POUND) CORNED BEEF BRISKET
1 LARGE WHOLE ONION
3 CARROTS
2 STALKS CELERY
1 LARGE HEAD WHITE CABBAGE, CUT INTO $^1/_2$-INCH WEDGES

Soak the brisket overnight, covered in cold water. Remove brisket and place in a pot with fresh cold water, onion, carrots, and celery. Bring to a boil, lower heat, and simmer slowly for 3 $^1/_2$ to 4 $^1/_2$ hours, adding water as necessary to keep the meat covered. The brisket is done when it can be pierced easily with a fork.

Lift the brisket out of the pot, place on a cookie sheet or in a large shallow pan, and place in a 300° F oven for 25 minutes. Meanwhile, steam the cabbage wedges in the brisket cooking liquid until tender but not mushy, 10 to 15 minutes. Remove the meat to a slicing board and trim off the excess fat. Slice and serve with the cabbage wedges.

*J*ack Haley and his wife with Jack Haley, Jr. The Haleys shared a happy family moment before dinner at the Beverly Hills Derby. Jack Haley, who had been a comedian in vaudeville and on the stage, will always be remembered as the Tin Man in Mervyn LeRoy's *The Wizard of Oz*. His son, Jack, Jr., married Liza Minelli, the daughter of Judy Garland, another visitor to the land of Oz. In 1974 Jack Haley, Jr., exposed a new generation of fans to Hollywood's glorious past when he wrote, directed, and produced *That's Entertainment*, the tribute to MGM musicals.

𝔍rene Hervey, Allan Jones, and their daughter Gayle
A popular Hollywood couple, lovely actress Irene Hervey and her husband, Allan Jones, brought their daughter Gayle to the Brown Derby for lunch in 1938. Their son, Jack Jones, has carried on the show business tradition as a recording star and in nightclub appearances all over the world. Jack was born at three in the morning just after his father finished the first recording session of "Donkey Serenade," which became his biggest hit and sold more than two million copies. Allan was also a romantic singing star on-screen in *Showboat* (1936) and *The Boys from Syracuse*, which also featured Irene.

Allan Jones

Esther Williams with sons Ben Gage, Jr. (left), and Kimball (right) at daughter Susan's christening party

Sally Cobb and Wisconsin's Governor Kohler

Esther Williams, MGM's glamorous swimming star, also devoted herself to children's charities. In 1955, as chairman of the children's wing of the City of Hope Medical Center, I presented Esther with a plaque to honor her as Hollywood's Mother of the Year. We went on to work together with visually handicapped children and Esther continues teaching blind children to swim in a program she started forty years ago. Esther's graceful style was showcased in the spectacular production numbers of *Neptune's Daughter*, *Million Dollar Mermaid*, and many other musicals in the 1940s and 1950s.

When Esther and Ben Gage's daughter Susan was christened in early 1954, Governor Kohler and I were her godparents. The Brown Derby created elaborate Candy Ribbon Cakes for the occasion. The "ribbon" was actually thin glistening hard candy. The spectacular cakes were the specialty of the Derby's famous pastry chef, Rudolph Frederick, whom Bob Cobb brought from Germany in 1931. Bob had these cakes made specially for each of Esther's children—Susan's was the traditional pink, Ben's was blue, and Kim's was a green and white stripe.

Shirley Temple

In 1939, The Brown Derby's famed pastry chef, Frederick, prepared the cake for the official celebration of Shirley Temple's tenth birthday. Shirley's enormous popularity sometimes made it difficult to be out in public but Shirley and her parents—and her chauffeur-bodyguard—often dined at the Hollywood Brown Derby. Although other restaurants have claimed to have invented the non-alcoholic Shirley Temple "cocktail", it actually originated at the Brown Derby. It became so popular that Bob Cobb, who was a cowboy from Montana, began making the Roy Rogers "cocktail" for boys.

After leaving Hollywood and the movies when she married Charles Black in 1950, Shirley Temple Black returned to the Hollywood Brown Derby with her son Charles Jr. in 1959.

εarl Ebi, Bob Cobb, Edgar Bergen, Sidney Strotz
In May 1946 Bob hosted a lunch for Edgar Bergen and his friends to celebrate the birth of Bergen's daughter Candice. The proud father happily passed out cigars. Edgar's wife, Frances Westerman, was a beautiful former model and the popularity of Edgar Bergen and Charlie McCarthy was at its peak—the Hollywood press announced the happy arrival of "Charlie's sister."

Claude Stroud, Gloria Brewster, Clarence Stroud, Barbara Brewster
Edgar Bergen's radio show featured the Stroud twins, Claude and Clarence. The publicity department at Twentieth Century-Fox arranged their meeting with the Brewster twins over lunch at the Beverly Hills Derby in 1936. The beautiful Brewster twins, Barbara and Gloria, contract players at the studio, went on to star with the Strouds in the feature short "Double Trouble." Later on, the Brewsters performed on Broadway and Barbara met and married Alfred Bloomingdale, the show's producer and the grandson of the founder of the department store that bears his name. They divorced after two years and Bloomingdale married Betsy Newling, who became the international hostess, Betsy Bloomingdale. Barbara has been happily married ever since to Bob Lemond. The most enduring result of the twin's lunch at the Derby was the 1939 marriage of Gloria and Claude, which lasted forty-six years.

oy Rogers and Dale Evans
Roy Rogers, "The King of the Cowboys," and
Dale Evans were married on New Year's Eve,
1947. Roy Rogers is truly as American as
apple pie. Roy had proposed to Dale while he
was riding Trigger, "the smartest horse in the
movies." After their first picture together, *The*

Brown Derby Apple Pie

SERVES 6

The Brown Derby chefs spent two years, $10,000, and baked hundreds of pies before they found the perfect Apple Pie. This recipe with its famous home-made flavor is baked with Jonathan and Winesap apples from Washington.

2 CUPS THINLY SLICED APPLES (1 CUP JONATHAN AND 1 CUP WINESAP)
$^3/_8$ CUP WHITE SUGAR
$^3/_8$ CUP BROWN SUGAR
1 TABLESPOONS ALL-PURPOSE FLOUR
$^1/_8$ TEASPOON CINNAMON

$^1/_{16}$ TEASPOON NUTMEG
PINCH OF SALT
BROWN DERBY PASTRY FOR APPLE PIE (SEE BELOW)
2 TABLESPOONS MELTED BUTTER, COOLED

Preheat the oven to 450°F. Mix apples and seasonings together. Roll out half the pastry and fit it into an 8-inch pan, leaving about 1 inch overhanging. Brush bottom and sides with melted butter. Add apple mixture and dot with melted butter. If apples are dry, add water as needed to moisten; roll out a second round of pastry and lay it over the apples. Crimp together the top and bottom layers of pastry and flute the edges. Bake 20 minutes. Lower the heat to 350°F and bake 40 minutes longer, or until the top is golden brown and the apples are tender. Cool free from draft.

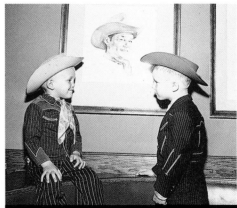

*R*oy Rogers, Jr. ("Dusty") and Harry John David Rogers ("Sandy")

Dusty and Sandy beside the charcoal portrait of their father, Roy Rogers, at the Los Feliz Brown Derby. Portraits of all the great cowboys and their horses lined the walls of the Los Feliz dining room in the 1950s: Tom Mix and Tony, Gene Autry and Champion, and of course Roy Rogers and Trigger. Roy's love of children was what attracted Dale most about the singing cowboy when they first met. Together they raised nine children.

1950s

*L*aurence Olivier and Vivien Leigh

The most famous theater couple in the world returned to the Brown Derby in 1950 after being away from Hollywood for almost nine years. They were also now Sir Laurence and Lady Olivier and the press coverage was considerable. The couple had been lovers for years when Vivien arrived in Hollywood to test for *Gone with the Wind*. Olivier had already come over from England to film *Wuthering Heights*, but they were both married and the morals of 1939 required secrecy. This photograph was taken in August 1950, when filming began on *A Streetcar Named Desire*. Leigh's portrayal of Blanche DuBois won her a second Oscar.

Black Bottom Pie

SERVES 6 TO 8

Vivien Leigh's favorite dessert during the filming of *Gone with the Wind* was the Brown Derby's sensational Black Bottom Pie.

2 TEASPOONS UNFLAVORED GELATIN

$^1/_2$ CUP MILK

$1^1/_2$ TABLESPOONS SUGAR

1 PINCH SALT

1 TEASPOON VANILLA EXTRACT

1 EGG YOLK

3 OUNCES SWEET CHOCOLATE

2 CUPS HEAVY CREAM

1 PREBAKED 10-INCH PIE SHELL

Soak gelatin in small amount of cold water for 15 minutes. Bring milk just to boiling point. Beat together sugar, salt, $^1/_2$ teaspoon vanilla, and egg yolk until light, thick, and creamy. While whisking, add $^1/_2$ of the milk to the egg mixture. Blend well, then return egg mixture to remaining hot milk. Return the custard to the heat, stirring constantly, for a few seconds; do not let it come close to boiling. Add the gelatin to the hot mixture, stirring until completely dissolved; strain the mixture through a very fine sieve. Shave 2 ounces of the chocolate and add it to the mixture; beat until smooth. Cool the mixture until it reaches creamlike consistency.

Whip cream and fold half of it into the chocolate mixture along with the remaining $^1/_2$ teaspoon vanilla. Fill prebaked pie shell with the mixture and place in refrigerator for 30 minutes. Spread the remaining whipped cream about 1 inch thick over the pie. Dust with grated chocolate.

𝓕rank Sinatra and Ava Gardner

Ava Gardner appeared with Frank Sinatra during a rally for Adlai Stevenson at the Hollywood Palladium wearing the mink stole Frank had given her as an engagement present. Later, when Frank and Ava entered the Hollywood Brown Derby for dinner, everyone in the room felt the electricity between them. Ava was billed as "the world's most beautiful animal" in *The Barefoot Contessa*. Sinatra said that "she isn't just beautiful, Ava is the most beautiful woman in the world." Their public affair caused a sensation in the press. Of their brief and stormy marriage Ava later wrote: "We could never understand why it hadn't and couldn't work out."

Mickey Rooney

*a*va Gardner and Mickey Rooney

Mickey Rooney and Ava Gardner, shown here in the Bamboo Room for a late supper, often stopped at the Derby when making the rounds in Hollywood. Ava met Mickey on her very first day as a contract player at MGM in 1941. He was filming *Babes on Broadway* with Judy Garland and was the most popular star in America. Ava was nineteen and Mickey was just two years older when they asked Louis B. Mayer for his permission to marry. With the studio approval that was required under their contracts, they were married on January 10, 1942. One year later the marriage was over.

Ronald and Nancy Reagan

Shortly before the birth of their son Ron in 1958, the Reagans dined at the Hollywood Brown Derby. Still a leading man, Ronnie had costarred with his wife a year earlier in *Hellcats of the Navy*. Nancy was an actress when they were married but gave up her career to be a wife and mother. Their wedding in 1952 had been a private ceremony at the Little Brown Church of the Valley with their friends William Holden and his wife, Brenda Marshall, serving as best man and matron of honor.

Jimmy Durante

A Brown Derby regular almost from the restaurant's beginning, Durante clowned with an unidentified young woman when the original *Brown Derby Cookbook* was published in 1949. The great "Schnozzola" first came to Hollywood in 1930 and began his film career at MGM. He went on to become a major star on radio and later enjoyed the greatest success of his extraordinary career on television with "The Jimmy Durante Show" (1954–57). Before or after virtually every show, Durante came into the Derby, usually with members of his production team.

Durante was the only celebrity whose caricature required two frames. His inscription read: "Get me back in that other frame (I mean my Schnozzola) Hot Cha,"

Corned Beef Hash

SERVES 10 TO 12

At the Brown Derbies the patties
were topped with a poached egg

1 POUND LEAN, EXTRA WELL-DONE CORNED
BEEF BRISKET
1 CUP DICED BOILED POTATOES
1 TABLESPOON FINELY CHOPPED SLIGHTLY
BROWNED ONIONS (OPTIONAL)
DASH OF PEPPER
2 TABLESPOONS BUTTER OR VEGETABLE OIL

Grind or chop corned beef very fine. Place in mixing bowl, add potatoes, onions and pepper, and combine well. If the mixture seems too dry add a small amount of cold water. Mold into 6-ounce patties and refrigerate for 2 hours. Remove from rerigerator and sauté in butter on both sides. Flip patties several times to attain a good crust.

irk Douglas

Douglas, pictured dining on the Brown Derby's Corned Beef Hash, became Hollywood's top male star after World War II in films such as *Champion* (1949) and *Lust for Life* (1956). Douglas was nominated for an Oscar three times but never won. However, his son Michael's first film as a producer, the classic *One Flew Over the Cuckoo's Nest*, won Best Picture in 1975. Michael went on to win Best Actor for his performance in Wall Street in 1987. In recent years, Kirk has become a writer, known particularly for his autobiography, *Ragman's Son*. Above all, though, he will be best remembered for his strong and determined on-screen presence.

Cobina Wright, Meredith Willson, Sally Cobb, Rene Willson
Nationally syndicated Hollywood columnist Cobina Wright
stopped to say hello when I was dining with Meredith Willson
and his charming wife, Rene. Table hopping yielded a great deal
of material for Cobina's column; she also conducted countless
interviews in the Brown Derby's leather booths. For decades the
Derby was the place for celebrities to be interviewed. Meredith
was a longtime friend of Bob's and mine. He spent many hours
with Bob in the Record Room discussing the musical he was
writing about the Iowa of his childhood. *The Music Man*
became a Broadway smash whose screen adaptation was
equally successful.

Don Ameche and Gail Patrick

In 1940, Don Ameche and Gail Patrick, who was then married to Bob Cobb, unveiled one of the nation's first television sets in the Bamboo Room. The American Society of Composers, Authors and Publishers (ASCAP) issued the first television license for the use of copyrighted music in the country to the Brown Derby Restaurant. The limited broadcasting schedule was Tuesdays and Thursdays, 2:30 to 3:30 P.M. and every evening except Sunday, 8:00 to 9:00 P.M; the public was invited to attend and to hear and see wrestling matches and fights from the American Legion Stadium in Hollywood, daytime games of the Hollywood Stars, and newsreels. The growth of the television industry was delayed until after the country recovered from World War II. In 1947 there were still only an estimated 350 television sets in Los Angeles.

𝒟inah Shore

Dinah Shore was a young singer from Tennessee when she came to Hollywood and found success as a recording artist. Shown here in 1941 while still a brunette, she mimicked William Powell's famous caricature in the Bamboo Room. The "Chevy Show Starring Dinah Shore" had its premiere on NBC in 1951. Dinah's singing and warm Southern charm endeared her to the American public and made her variety show a hit throughout the 1950s.

*G*roucho Marx and Red Skelton

Two of television's early stars clowned over lunch at the Hollywood Derby. Groucho's television version of his radio quiz show "You Bet Your Life" began in 1950 and became the highest rated show on television. Skelton, who also had been successful in radio and films began his long running "The Red Skelton Show" in 1953.

Groucho was a Derby regular for forty years. He was unpredictable and outrageous, especially when he was joined by his brothers Chico, Harpo, and Zeppo. When they were in the Derby together, their antics resembled their behavior in their great films, *A Night at the Opera* and *A Day at the Races*.

Brown Derby Rice Pudding

SERVES 6

Durante loved the Brown Derby Rice Pudding, one of our most popular desserts.

1 QUART MILK
$^1/_2$ TEASPOON SALT
1 TABLESPOON VANILLA EXTRACT
1 CINNAMON STICK
1 TEASPOON EACH ORANGE AND LEMON ZEST
4 TABLESPOONS LONG-GRAIN RICE
$^1/_2$ CUP RAISINS
3 TABLESPOONS SUGAR
2 EGG YOLKS
1 PINT WHIPPING CREAM
GROUND CINNAMON

In a heavy pot, bring the milk to a boil. Add salt, vanilla, cinnamon, orange and lemon zest, rice, and raisins. Simmer, covered, for 25 to 30 minutes or until rice is tender, stirring frequently. Beat the sugar and egg yolks together until they are quite thick and light yellow in color; stir in the cream. Add the egg mixture to the rice slowly, mixing thoroughly, and bring just to a simmer. Remove from heat and cool, stirring frequently, to room temperature. Divide the pudding among six 4-ounce ramekins and refrigerate if not being served immediately. Just before serving, preheat the broiler. Sprinkle the tops of the puddings with cinnamon and place under the heat to brown lightly.

The Record Room

The Record Room in the Hollywood Brown Derby

Hollywood's importance in the recording industry in 1954 was reflected in the ultra-modern Capital Records Building under construction on Vine Street and in the new Record Room in the Hollywood Brown Derby. The Record Room opened after a complete remodeling of what had been the fabled Bamboo Room. Pastel portraits of million-selling artists from Frank Sinatra and Doris Day to Elvis Presley lined the walls.

Tony Martin and Cyd Charisse
In the 1950s, singer Tony Martin and lovely Cyd Charisse
shared a late supper in the Hollywood Brown Derby's
Record Room. They have been happily married since 1948
when they were both stars at MGM. Tony's films include
Hit the Deck, with Debbie Reynolds, and *Easy to Love*,
with Esther Williams. Cyd is classically trained in ballet and
one of Hollywood's best dressed women. She performed
with elegance and ease opposite Hollywood's greatest
dancers: Gene Kelly in *Singin' in the Rain* and Fred Astaire
in Cole Porter's *Silk Stockings*.

Bob and Sally Cobb Greet Lucille Ball and Desi Arnaz

In 1955 the "I Love Lucy" show headed west when Lucy and Ricky and the Mertzes drove from New York to Hollywood. In the first episode of their mythical Hollywood vacation, Ricky goes to the movie studio while Lucy, Ethel, and Fred have lunch. Lucy decides to go to the famous Brown Derby in her search for movie stars because "tracking them down one by one takes so much time" and the Derby is "their watering hole." Bob gave a party to screen the episode for Lucy, Desi, the cast, and the press in the new private room at the Los Feliz Brown Derby. Over the years the episode became one of the best known, rerun hundreds of times on television.

Bob and Sally Cobb, Lucille Ball, Vivian Vance

Bob loved Lucy. And he loved Vivian Vance, too; we both did. It looks as though I was telling a joke here, but it was really Bob's wonderful sense of humor that always kept the party going.

Lucy, Bill Holden, William Frawley

In the episode, Lucy is thrilled when she spots Cary Grant across the dining room and then sees Eve Arden sitting in a booth beneath her caricature. But, it's William Holden who becomes the focus of Lucy's attention when he is seated in the next booth. As the scene goes on, Bill "turns the tables" on Lucy and stares back at her. Lucy becomes so flustered that she decides to leave, but not before showing us how to eat Spaghetti Derby.

Lucy and William Holden

Bill Holden hasn't even received his Cobb Salad when Lucy bumps into the waiter, causing him to spill his tray all over Bill in a classic moment of television slapstick.

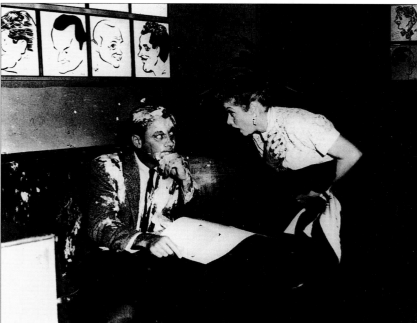

Norma Shearer, Ben Lyon, Marty Arrouge, Bebe Daniels, Bob Hope, Lorena Mayer, Irene Dunne, Louis B. Mayer

In 1954 Bob and I gave a party for Bebe Daniels, a big star in the 1920s and 1930s, and her equally famous husband, the actor Ben Lyon. The Lyons, married from 1930 until Bebe's death in 1971, had returned to the United States for a visit. Throughout most of their marriage they lived in England. During World War II, they were among America's most successful goodwill ambassadors.

Harold Lloyd

*L*ouella Parsons with Harold and Mildred Lloyd

The immortal silent-film comedian Harold Lloyd and his wife were among Bebe and Ben's many friends there that evening, although Louella overlooked mentioning them in her column.

*J*oan Crawford, Clark Gable, and Louella Parsons

Hollywood veterans Clark Gable, Joan Crawford and Louella Parsons were at a party in the American Room in the mid 1940s. Louella wrote that Gable was "still the great lover on and off the screen." When Gable and Crawford met on the set of *Dance Fools Dance* in 1930, Joan was a major star and Clark was a newcomer. Joan later said of Gable, "This magnetic man had more sheer animal magic than anyone in the world, and every woman knew it. The electricity between us sparked on the screen too. It wasn't just acting. We were madly in love." They made eight films together, including *Possessed* (1931) and *Dancing Lady* (1933). Crawford was married to Douglas Fairbanks, Jr., and Gable to his second wife, Ria. Their affair presented a potential public relations problem to MGM, where they both were under contract, and Louis B. Mayer ordered them to break it off. But they remained friends until Gable's death in 1961.

Stuffed Pork Chops California

SERVES 4

Joan Crawford always looked and acted the great movie star whenever she was in the Derby or out in public. A Mid-Westener, she loved hearty American cooking, especially the Brown Derby's stuffed pork chops.

4 (2-INCH-THICK) PORK CHOPS
SALT AND PEPPER
4 TABLESPOONS BUTTER
2 APPLES, PEELED, CORED, AND THINLY SLICED
1 MEDIUM ONION, CHOPPED
3 OUNCES RAISINS
1 CUP DRY BREAD CROUTONS
$1/4$ TEASPOON CELERY SALT
$1/4$ TEASPOON GROUND NUTMEG
$1/2$ CUP CHICKEN BROTH

Preheat the oven to 350° F. Split the meat side of each chop to the bone and fold open like a book. Pound both sides quite thin and season with salt and pepper. In a heavy skillet, heat butter over medium heat. Add apples and onions and brown lightly. Add raisins, croutons, celery salt, and nutmeg and sauté 10 minutes over low heat. Add chicken broth and blend well. Divide dressing evenly among the open pork chops, bring edges together, and secure them with toothpicks. Place chops in a single layer in a buttered baking pan and roast for 1 hour.

Betty Hutton, George Jessel, Governor Goodwin J. Knight

Vivacious Betty Hutton chatted with comedian George Jessel and California Governor, Goodwin J. Knight during a party she hosted at the Los Feliz Brown Derby in 1954. Cecil B. DeMille was also there that night. Betty was a favorite of DeMille's after her performance in his spectacular Academy Award-winning production, *The Greatest Show on Earth* (1952). Betty's diet for her physically demanding role as an aerialist in that film included a steak and a Cobb Salad in the Hollywood Derby each night after shooting at

Bob Hope

ℬob Hope

One of the most memorable parties was a Christmas dinner for the Santa Clauses of Hollywood. Bob Cobb heard a seventy-year-old actor who played Santa in Miracle on 34th Street lament that "there was no Christmas for Santa Claus," so Bob invited one hundred department-store Santas to join him for a Christmas feast at the Hollywood Derby. Bob Hope joined in to entertain the group, which included actors from the silent-screen era, young men working their way through college, and professional Santas. Of all the parties over the years at the Derby, this was one of Bob Cobb's favorites.

Baked Ham Brown Derby Style

SATURDAY SPECIAL OF THE DAY

SERVES 12 TO 15

A traditional holiday dinner at the Brown Derby featuring Baked Ham or Roast Turkey was enjoyed by many Californians, including Bob Hope's family. Bob and Dolores chose the American Room of the Derby for a large family gathering on Thanksgiving, before Bob went overseas on his annual Christmas tour in the 1950s.

1 (12-POUND) SMOKED HAM, SKINNED

36 WHOLE CLOVES

2 CUPS WHITE WINE

1 SMALL STICK CINNAMON

2 MEDIUM APPLES, QUARTERED

1 ORANGE, QUARTERED

1 CUP DRAINED CRUSHED PINEAPPLE

1 POUND BROWN SUGAR

Preheat the oven to 300°F. Remove any excess fat from the ham. Score the ham into squares with a cookie cutter or sharp knife and insert a clove into each square. Place the ham in a roasting pan. Add wine, cinnamon, apples, orange, pineapple, and 4 cups of water. Bake in the oven for 2 hours, basting every 20 minutes.

Spread the brown sugar over the top of the ham. Bake 1 hour longer, basting about every 10 minutes to glaze ham evenly. Add hot water if the liquid reduces significantly.

Note: This is a very simple dish to prepare, but the secret to success is basting often, which allows the fruity juices to infuse the ham with a delicious and full flavor. When the ham is fully cooked, the liquid should be reduced to a heavy syrup.

1960s

Terrace Room

*P*at Buttram, Hedda Hopper, Arthur Godfrey, Bob Cobb

Bob's old friends Hedda Hopper and Arthur Godfrey posed with Gene Autry's sidekick, Pat Buttram, outside the Brown Derby in 1963. Through the years, whenever Arthur Godfrey came to Los Angeles he would always call Bob. Godfrey was staying at the Bel Air Hotel. Since we lived just up from the hotel, Godfrey suggested that Bob come by that morning on his way to the Derby. Bob joined him for a breakfast that included Godfrey's customary Silver Fizz. The suite was wired for a national broadcast of Godfrey's radio show and Bob was introduced live—on the air—as the owner of the world-famous Brown Derby. We had just completed the first paperback edition of *The Brown Derby Cookbook*, and in an unintentionally generous offer (resulting from a Silver Fizz) Bob offered to send the book to any of Godfrey's fans who would like a copy. The calls started immediately and we needed to hire three secretaries to handle the thousands of requests for complimentary copies. Needless to say, I wasn't very happy.

1970

𝒩eil Reagan, Sally Cobb, Governor Ronald Reagan

The Reagan brothers and I were friends who shared more than three decades of memories when we had lunch during Ronald's second term as governor of California. Ronald and Neil were also known by the nick-names "Dutch" and "Moon," which had been given to them in childhood. Ronald often joined "Moon" for lunch at the Hollywood Derby—the first booth on the right was Neil Reagan's. Neil was one of the top advertising men in town and he ate in the Derby every day for years. Many of the big ad agencies were headquartered near Hollywood and Vine, and the executives all gathered at the Derby for the ritual two-martini lunch.

Neil was with the McCann Ericson agency, which handled General Electric—for which his brother had been the spokesman—and The Carnation Company, whose president, Dwight Stuart, was frequently at the table. Dwight and his beautiful wife, the former actress Kathleen Gallant, were prominent in Los Angeles society.

Paul and Della Williams, Marilyn and Elbert Hudson, Mervyn LeRoy, Sally Cobb, Mark Taper

It was a nostalgic dinner at the Hollywood Brown Derby honoring the renowned architect Paul R. Williams, the first African-American member and fellow of the American Institute of Architects. Mr. Williams and I met in 1939 on my first trip to California at a lovely dinner party by Jules Stein, the founder of MCA, and his wife, Doris. A major topic of conversation was the new MCA headquarters (now the Litton Building), which Williams had designed. The next day we toured the elegant Georgian structure in Beverly Hills. When we returned to Kansas City, I invited Mr. Williams for a visit to discuss his designs for the new house we were planning in Brentwood, California. My friendship that began over fifty years ago with Paul and Della Williams continues today with their granddaughter, the author Karen Hudson. Among Paul Williams's many extraordinary contributions to Los Angeles architecture are the newly restored Beverly Hills Hotel and numerous celebrity residences, including those of Barbara Stanwyck and Frank Sinatra.

*B*y the 1970s Hollywood had changed dramatically as the entertainment inducstry moved to other parts of the Los Angeles area. In 1975 The Brown Derby Corporation was sold to Walter Scharfe and Elisabeth Khittl-Scharfe. Walter, a marketing expert from German, was well aware of the Brown Derby's international reputation and he and his wife worked hard to maintain the restaurant's tradition. The Hollywood Brown Derby continued operation until 1985 when it was closed for earthquake reconstruction. The historic building was demolished in 1994 after further earthquake damage.

On what would have been the Brown Derby's sixty-fifth birthday, February 14, 1994, a memorial service was held on the site. The Derby's loyal public and members of the press paid tribute to the glory that was once the Hollywood Brown Derby.

Today the legend of the Brown Derby lives on in two new locations. The restaurant, complete with copies of the original caricatures, has been recreated in Disney World at the Disney-MGM Studios theme park and at the spectacular MGM Grand Hotel in Las Vegas.

Gracie Allen, George Burns,
Mary Livingstone, Jack Benny
leaving the Hollywood Brown
Derby's Bamboo Room, circa 1939.

$\mathcal{A}$ c k n o w l e d g m e n t s

THE AUTHORS WANT to thank the many people who generously shared their memories of the Brown Derby during the process of writing this book, with special thanks to the following institutions and individuals.

Robert H. Cobb Collection

Academy of Motion Picture Arts and Sciences/Margaret Herrick Library, Georgia Aldworth, Army Archerd, Sid Avery and Ron Avery/Motion Picture & Television Photo Archive, Marjory Bentley, Nat Dallinger, John Engstead, David Gill Evans, Bern Hebert, Jean Howard, Karen E. Hudson, Gregg Hunter, Somi Kim, Jerome Lawrence, Mark Santa Maria, Andrew Midgely, Wally Seawell, Walter P. Scharfe, Marc Wanamaker/Bison Archives, Marjorie Walker, James Watters, Jeff Wettleson, Lorraine Wild

The authors also want to express their gratitude to Jane Wyman for her gracious tribute to Bob Cobb and his beloved Brown Derby.

Index of Patrons

About the Authors

Sally Wright Cobb was married to Bob Cobb, the owner of the Brown Derby, for twenty-five years and ran the restaurant after his death in 1970.

Mark Willems, a graduate of the University of Minnesota, is a writer with a love of Hollywood who lives in Los Angeles. He is also a recognized artist whose work has been exhibited in New Orleans and Los Angeles and is represented in collections throughout the United States.

Index of Caricatures

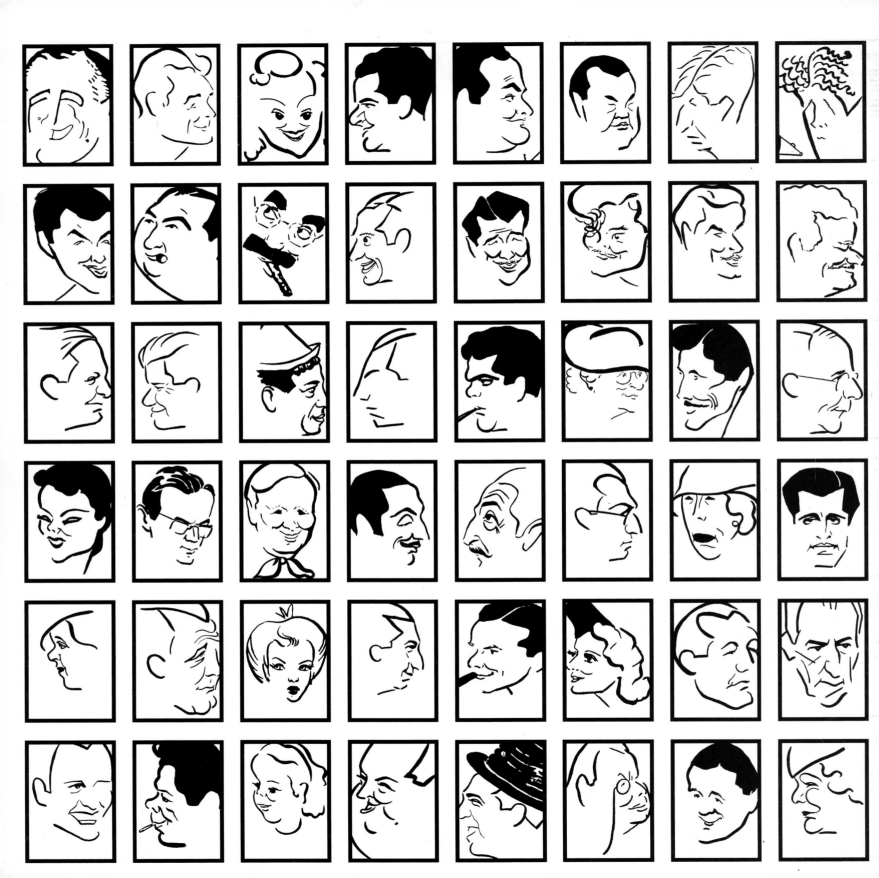